How to Make Better Decisions by Asking Yourself Better Questions

MARTIN GOODYER

Crown House Publishing Limited

www.crownhouse.co.uk

First published by

Crown House Publishing Ltd
Crown Buildings, Bancyfelin, Carmarthen, Wales, SA33 5ND, UK
www.crownhouse.co.uk

and

Crown House Publishing Company LLC
PO Box 2223, Williston, VT 05495
www.crownhousepublishing.com

British Library Cataloguing-in-Publication Data
A catalogue entry for this book is available
from the British Library.

Print ISBN 978-178583031-0
Mobi ISBN 978-178583169-0
ePub ISBN 978-178583170-6
ePDF ISBN 978-178583171-3

LCCN 2015953356

Printed and bound in the UK by
Gomer Press, Llandysul, Ceredigion

Acknowledgements

Thank you to everyone who has made me ask the question that would eventually lead to the writing of this book. Including, but not limited to:

- The Latin teacher who, instead of introducing me to keys that might unlock the secrets of the long forgotten past, insisted I learn six ways to say 'table', with no hint of where that might lead – thanks for that.
- The 'friends' who helped me lose most of the 1980s in a haze of bonhomie and red wine – I hope you enjoyed it because I can't really recall.
- The 'parental figure' who suggested to an impressionable boy that an intellectually un-stimulating career would yield greater success than a challenging one – nice one, it only took me eighteen years to realise I shouldn't be there!
- … and everyone else who contributed to me eventually becoming a psychologist and then enrolling me as my first 'subject'. Thank you all, I couldn't have got here without you.

It's all very well to say that anything worth doing is worth the pain of doing it, but when that pain is shared by the people closest to the doer, then due credit must be paid to those who sometimes suffered in silence … and were often less quiet about it!

So, thank you to Rachel for your ideas, your support and your 'putting up with me' through the writing process. Thanks too to my good friend Jason, without whom the concept of this book would never have been born, and to all my loved ones, without whom I'd have much less to write about. I could never have made it to the end of this book without the love of my wife Rachel and my incredibly supportive family. Every day I wake up and think, 'WTF? How did I get so lucky?!'

Contents

Foreword

I first met Martin Goodyer in Hawaii back in 1998 at a nine-day intensive programme run by Anthony Robbins. What struck me instantly was not only Martin's extremely personable nature, but also his unique ability to *want* to coach effectively. There were many in our team at the event who had arrived at Tony's event needing some help, in one area of their life or another. Martin, it seemed, was there for much the same reason I found myself there – curiosity, and an open mind to learn new teaching techniques. Martin is one of life's sponges: he absorbs information for fun, and his memory retention is akin to that of Stephen Fry! What I noticed early on was the second anyone in the group had a problem, Martin was instantly there, doing whatever he could to coach them out of their negative thought process and/or situation. It came as no surprise, then, when Martin went on to make 'effective coaching' his vocation and, inadvertently, his career.

Not a life bus!

The reason I keep emphasising 'effective coaching' is because anyone can, and often seemingly does, call themselves a coach – usually of the life kind. Many of these people are more 'life bus' than 'life coach'! Martin is not just a coach; he is one of the most effective coaches I know, and that is the key word here: effective. He is paid extremely well by blue-chip companies because he knows how to get people to take action. However, as wonderful as he is when he works with companies to bring harmony with workers and increase productivity, I feel where Martin comes into his own is when he works one-to-one with someone. This is why I am extremely pleased Martin has written this book. We all have 'WTF just happened?' moments (I love the title of the book, by the way – but then I would say that, as I had a hand in coming up with it) but, as Martin says:

> It's not the 'WTF just happened?' moment that defines you, but rather what you do with that 'WTF just happened?' moment.

Although many of the actual 'WTF just happened?' moments in this book are unique to the individuals, every single one has coaching at the end which can be applied to a plethora of situations. The key is to read all of this book for the reason just stated, even if you feel a particular story has no relevance to your 'WTF just happened?' situation. The book is a form of 'conscious hypnosis' and shouldn't be over-analysed, but simply absorbed. I had the privilege of being on the same Channel 4 TV show as Martin, *The Fit Farm*, for five weeks – and now you have the privilege of having him as your coach for the duration of this book – and perhaps beyond.

So sit back, kick off your shoes, and make a nice cuppa (or fresh juice!). However bad your situation may seem at this moment, you will either feel very differently about it by the end of the book, or you'll at least have the tools to get yourself into a better place.

Jason Vale
Author of twelve bestselling books on health, juicing and addiction, and documentary film producer of *Super Juice Me! The Big Juice Experiment*

How to avoid missing the point

WTF just happened to those 'opportunities to learn'?

We have all had 'WTF just happened?' moments – moments when your stomach turns over and you ask yourself what the heck just happened. That feeling when you teeter on the tightrope of life, wondering, 'Now what?' They are those moments when confidence eludes you, the unexpected stops you in your tracks, or when you step back and wonder, 'What the heck am I doing here?' These moments are pivotal as they can simultaneously be horribly gut-churning and yet provide amazing clarity; they may momentarily shake your self-belief but then, because you always get to make a better decision afterwards, be a cause for celebration as you use the opportunity to grow.

Like, for instance, the time I was invited to speak at a conference and thought it might be just the opportunity I'd been waiting for. I was so excited because I was to address a packed audience in an actual theatre. Not some boring hotel conference room or lecture theatre, but a real honest to goodness theatre with a balcony and everything. I arrived on the morning of the talk and while being escorted to the 'green room' was told that every one of the six-hundred seats was to be occupied.

'Wow,' I thought, 'this is going to be amazing!' Yet, amazing is not quite how I'd describe the experience.

Did I suck? Was that the problem? Well, I'm not sure, I hope not but it was hard to tell. You see, that particular 'WTF just happened?' moment occurred a few seconds after leaving the stage in stony silence, having watched helplessly as one after the other a steady stream of people walked out of the auditorium during my address. It was dreadful, and nothing like this had ever happened before. I'd always had pretty good feedback and people tended to like what I had to say, so what on earth had happened?

With profound apologies the organiser of the event informed me that the whole audience had been made up of teachers, and that today was the first day of a new term and new school year. He might have mistaken my frozen bemused smile for reassurance because he went on to admit that none of them had known they were being loaded onto coaches and shipped off to the theatre to be told how best to motivate people. He noted that, in hindsight, it might have been better to have advised them in advance and to have at least sorted out their timetables before organising a regional event. He thought that perhaps they weren't quite in the right mood to be motivated to listen to a talk on motivation. No kidding!

After he'd gone and I sat there alone in the deserted green room, I asked myself, 'WTF just happened?' How had I allowed myself to get into that position? Of course I could have had a hissy-fit and gone all 'diva' on the organisers but what good would that have done me? To be fair, I was tempted but managed to step away from it and take a deep breath and ask myself the question again, 'WTF just happened?' Cutting a long story short, I realised that the problem was mine in that a speaker should always know their audience. Therefore, the failure was mine, not because what I had to say wasn't good but because I had allowed my ego to get carried away with speaking to a full theatre rather than asking, 'How come the theatre is going to be full?' It was a lesson learned and one I have never forgotten. In fact, as I write this, more than a decade and a half after the event, it still causes me to wince with embarrassment. But it also reminds me that without asking the 'right' question, or at least a better question, another one of those 'WTF just happened?' moments might be right around the corner.

Asking better questions is important: it is a concept as well as an action. The assumption that when something happens it causes a person to behave in this way or that is flawed, because if when something happens it causes a person to think instead of respond, then the outcome is likely to change. Imagine you are driving on a motorway and ahead you see a stationary line of traffic. Many people will respond to this by cursing their bad luck and fretting about the prospect of being late at their destination. However, some will not jump to the conclusion that they are caught in a situation that inevitably means something bad. A few years ago I coached a lady who had to commute using the M25 motorway: a road that is notorious for traffic hold-ups, and her response to them had been to become stressed and agitated. There was very little she could do about traffic on the M25, but there was a lot she could do about her own thinking. Instead of rushing headlong into negative thoughts about being late, she was encouraged to stamp on her mental brakes and put a break in her thinking. It had transpired during the coaching that one of her goals was to spend time living in Italy and that learning to speak Italian was important to her, and yet despite wanting to learn she felt unable to dedicate time to it. She had tried using audio programmes in the car but was always distracted by driving, until the day she put in that mental break and asked herself a better question. Instead of unconsciously asking herself something along the lines of 'Why me?' or 'Why does this always have to happen?' she asked 'Is there any way I can use this time in a way I'd enjoy?'

To cut a long story short, she used the stationary and semi-stationary periods to engage with Italian audio language training and started having fun learning to speak Italian. In fact she started having so much fun that, in her words, 'It was very funny. I went from being frustrated about traffic to getting slightly miffed when the traffic started moving again!' Asking a better question is all about recognising that every one of us asks ourselves questions all the time, but we don't necessarily realise we are doing it. Sometimes those questions are useful and unfortunately very often they are not. Negative or self-limiting questions are a mental knee-jerk reaction to events, but are not the only choice of reaction open to us. If we raise our awareness of our own capability and of the possibility that always exists to just stop what we were about to ask, and start asking a question that is more helpful – a better question, then the chances are we'll get a better result.

I do enjoy learning and yet would prefer to only have to learn once. One 'WTF just happened?' moment is enough for anyone, which is why learning from somebody else's is preferable to having many more myself. If that is true for me, I guess it might be true for you too.

In almost twenty years of being a coaching psychologist, I've heard just about everything, and as well as helping my clients, I have also laughed, shed a private tear and learned a lot from them along the way. I've also noticed that some stories are repeated over and over: different people show up with much the same tale, and I wonder for a moment if it's déjà vu, but it's not. I've come to the conclusion that it must be a reflection of our times, or our society, or something else that's common among people. So all the stories in this book are about people like you and me. They're common to all of us because we've *all* had those moments when suddenly a voice in our head screams: 'WTF just happened?' It may not have happened to you yet, or if it has, it might not have been exactly like this – but it'll be pretty close.

I have to warn you – most of these stories don't have happy endings. They are not fairy tales, nor are they fables with deep hidden meanings; they are stories about losers. That's right, losers – people who have failed to win, missed their opportunity, or lost the plot. I tell them here because their misfortune gives you a chance to avoid a similar fate.

After crashing and burning in her new job, Imogen has never been the same.

Akiko allowed a boss who wasn't up to his job to ruin her career.

Alan convinced himself he was a loser and then proved himself right.

Andy is still broke, and Barry cursed his way through cancer.

Bev gave her love to a man who didn't share her preferences, while Carolyn lost everything she owned and sacrificed everything she'd been blessed with.

Christine got stuck in a fashion time warp, and Daphne wasted her talents and opportunities altogether.

Dean screwed up his life, and now it's too late to claw it back.

Helen got fired.

Ian lost his mojo.

Johnny still can't accept he is who he is.

Jan forgot to act on her plans until it was too late.

Karen and Michael did a great job of messing up parenthood, and Leroy was a loser when he really should have won.

Lisa was fat and couldn't seem to lose weight.

Luca has to live a life full of regrets that he can never put right.

It turned out to be a surprise for Neil that he didn't have any friends.

Oliver's reputation went down the toilet, along with all his cash.

Reece ended up paying off huge debts for years.

Rupal got leapfrogged by her junior staff member.

And poor old Steve – well, he got dumped.

Even after everything that had happened to her, Tina was still a doormat and a scammer's dream, while Tony spent years torturing himself because he made one silly mistake, and the otherwise very capable Victoria ended up trembling when she should have triumphed.

They are all losers but their stories offer you the chance to learn from their mistakes.

In among the gloom and doom, there are a few examples of how a WTF moment can lead to joy. These little rays of sunshine are intended to suggest that when you do more of whatever these people did, you too can feel the warmth. Those who are not losers, but who could so easily have been, have stories that might just inspire you to avoid the same pitfalls. They include Alison, who managed to ditch self-pity; Derek, who got over himself by asking better questions; Jenni and Albert, who seized their opportunities with both hands; and finally John, who quite simply did what he needed to do to be rich. Those WTF moments are ones to savour.

You may have noticed that there are more losers than winners. That's because this book is mainly made up of losers' stories; it's not a self-help book. The self-help bit is up to you.

At the end of each story there are some 'take-aways', but it's not a 'do this and you shall succeed' type of book – it's more of a 'don't do this and you might not fail quite so badly as these suckers' kind of book. Here's why: self-help books are OK, but many are not great. They normally tell you to do this or that and then you'll be fine – but having someone tell you to do this or do that is all well and good when you're tucked up in bed with time to read, but when it comes to real life – well … it's not like that, is it? Stuff happens, and by the time it's happened then it's too late to climb under the duvet and read about what you should have done. You can't do it again; it's too late. Good advice is only useful if you can remember to use it. Unfortunately (if you are anything like me), you may not remember all that good advice until it's too late. That's why this is a book of stories that illustrate how easy it is to alter the course of your own life and avoid too many WTF moments.

We all love a good story, don't we? You've only got to look at Disney to see that. Here's a quick quiz for you. (1) Which is the most important source of information for the public, Disney films or the BBC World Service? (2) How many Disney stories can you recall? (3) How many BBC World Service stories do you remember? For 'BBC World Service', you could substitute any reputable news source, and you may be able to recall recent news reports, but how many of those are as lasting as *The Little Mermaid*, *The Jungle Book* or the rest of the Disney catalogue? You won't be surprised when I tell you that most people agree that news sources are probably a more important information source, or that most people recall more Disney stories in detail than they do information about the state of the world. This is not because they value children's stories more than hard news, but because stories are easier to remember than facts. Facts may be more important, but stories stick in your brain. The stories in this book will stick with you. When you read them, you may find yourself asking 'How could this person not see what was going on?' or 'How stupid can people be?'

When it comes to those 'WTF just happened?' moments, it's likely that any information that might have protected you will have come from a news story rather than an animated tale. Most of these moments are painful, but you can recover from them.

Then there are some that are both difficult and painful at the time, and are also difficult and painful to learn from. For example:

In 2014 a father left his teenage son playing on his computer, posting on social media sites with his schoolmates. The father came home a short time later to find his son's computer open and online, but no sign of his son. Worried, he searched for the boy, and found him at the end of their garden. The boy had committed suicide. An online spat had escalated into something more serious, and the boy felt unable to cope, which led to him taking his own life.

I can't think of any story more devastating than this. His distraught parents went on to help other parents by urging them to pay attention to news reports about the way young people use the internet and social media. Even in their grief, they want other parents to pay attention and use what they hear, so that they don't have to suffer a similar loss.

You'll be pleased to know, I hope, that the WTF moments I'm bringing to your attention are nowhere near as horrific as this one, but they do sometimes feature death. This is because time is finite; none of us have as much time as we might think, and death just happens to play a big part in everyone's life – there's no getting away from that.

Useful information will stick with you, and will help you avoid the pain of regret when you recognise that a story is relevant to you, and time is relevant to us all. If you can feel some empathy with other people who've had their WTF moment, then this might just prevent you from having a similar one yourself. If your empathetic feelings are strong enough, then they will have as powerful an effect as if you'd actually had the WTF moment yourself. I bet that if you have a teenage child and aren't already monitoring their internet and social media usage, after reading those few lines, you probably will now: a similar effect will happen with every one of the moments in this book as long as I can stimulate an 'ugh' or 'oh no' or 'argh!' from you. Even those behaviours that you can't imagine yourself changing will change as soon as you decide they need to change.

For example, I used to love chocolate cake. Death by Chocolate cake with lashings of butter icing was my absolute favourite, until the day I bit into a slice made with rancid butter. It was an 'ugh' moment! My mouth moved faster than my brain, and before my brain had registered that this stuff tasted vile, I'd already swallowed some. In seconds I felt nauseous. It took weeks before I got the taste out of my mouth, and I could still smell the foul, nasty stuff even though I'd rinsed and rinsed with mouthwash and brushed my teeth. Even now, when I think of chocolate cake my first unconscious reaction keeps me from eating it. Of course, intellectually I know that a fresh slice of cake will taste lovely, but emotionally my body remembers the 'ugh' moment. It's enough to take chocolate cake off my personal menu.

The point is this: if you are to avoid ever saying 'WTF just happened?' your brain needs to move faster than your mouth! I don't want to make you sick but, like the chocolate cake with rancid butter icing, potential 'WTF just happened?' moments, once tasted, are more likely to be remembered.

Enjoy – and I hope these stories are as useful to you as they have been to me.

PS: A word or two about confidentiality

Here's the thing: I am an absolute stickler for confidentiality. However, I know that people learn by hearing stories. So, I have squared this circle by ensuring that the stories in this book, while true in essence, are not to be taken at face value, as I have changed more than just the names in them. Yet, interestingly, they apply to so many of the thousands of people I've met that it would be easy to say, 'That's about me!' Be assured it's not. It's not based on you, nor is it intended to specifically reflect your story. You may have shared some or all of the experiences of Daphne, Alan, Johnny or any of the other characters in this book, but they are not you, your confidentiality is intact, and unless you go around pointing out similarities between the people in here and your own story, then no one will be any the wiser.

How to avoid being embarrassed by being overheard

WTF just happened to my private conversation that no one else was ever supposed to hear?

Tony was angry - really, really angry. But who was he angry with? All will soon become clear, I promise. This isn't a tale of anger over good sense; it's about frustration trumping awareness and causing an otherwise careful, smart individual to miss something simple, something that on any other occasion he would have done without thinking, but because his capacity for thinking was all wrapped up with anger, he simply missed it. How can missing one simple everyday thing cause such a big issue? Frustration and/or anger are such strong emotions that they take up conscious thinking space and, when that happens, mistakes are almost bound to follow. Tony's mistake started because of frustration and ended with him getting really angry - with himself.

Tony and Gemma were on their way to the company annual conference. As managing director of the business Tony had established twenty years before and company secretary, respectively, as well as being a married couple, they weren't just the figureheads of their growing organisation; they were the heart and soul of it. They'd just come from a particularly tough board meeting and were looking forward to letting

9

their hair down at the pre-conference dinner. From the first year, when Tony had taken Gemma and their three employees out to dinner and toasted the successes they'd achieved, the dinner had grown into a more formal celebration of the past year – there were formal presentations of long service awards, training certificates and outstanding service awards. Tony and Gemma looked forward to it and hoped that the two hundred or so people who they now employed did too.

Just as they weren't afraid to reward success within the business, Tony and Gemma weren't shy about sharing in that success too. Having watched just one episode of *The Apprentice*, Tony had decided that if Lord Alan Sugar felt comfortable being seen in a brand-new Rolls-Royce, then so could he. Lord Sugar and Tony hailed from the same neck of the woods, and both had achieved their success without the help of any silver spoons. So Tony got over his fears of being seen as too flashy and got himself something similar – and he loved it! However, unlike the 'bear of the boardroom', who'd sit in his chauffeur-driven Roller, deciding who was going to hear the words 'You're fired!' this week, Tony opted for a sportier Bentley he could drive himself. Well, why wouldn't he? He'd earned it – no one in the company thought any less of him because of it, and it didn't do any of their collective self-esteem any harm.

So Tony and Gemma were cruising along the M4 enjoying the comforts of a beautifully made motor car, chatting.

'What did you think?' asked Tony.

Gemma replied, 'It's OK, I suppose, but he really could have done better.'

'I agree. Evan is a capable guy, but he dropped the ball on this one, and at his salary I expect more. You know, he gets paid almost ten grand more than Sharon but she's done a much better job lately.'

'Perhaps you should promote her and move Evan somewhere else?'

'Yeah, maybe ... but I don't want to forget that he has been loyal ... it's just he can be an idiot sometimes. I'm sure he hasn't done it on purpose. You know, he's better than the job he's doing, and it's really frustrating.'

'I know what you mean. It must be frustrating for Sharon too. Has she said anything to you?'

'Matter of fact, she did. She danced around it a bit because obviously she doesn't want Evan to think she's gone behind his back or anything, but she's as frustrated with him as I am.'

'What did you tell her?'

'Oh, I gave the proper company line ... you know, I have absolute faith in Evan, yada yada ... I will speak to him about it ... blah, blah.'

'OK. How did you leave it with her?'

'That was it, really, but she's probably expecting me to have a chat with Evan soon.'

'I hope she doesn't get too frustrated and leave.'

'Yeah, me too. At the moment she's worth about two of Evan, so losing her would be a real shame ...'

'It would be worse than that – it'd be a disaster at the moment ...'

Their conversation drifted to home and the children and domestic matters, and then they arrived at the hotel.

Behind them was Evan's people carrier. He, Sharon, and three members of their marketing team had been following Tony's Bentley all the way from the office. The thing is, when they set off, Tony had rung Evan on his mobile to confirm the address of the hotel they were going to. After their call, which had been on speakerphone, Tony hadn't pushed the button to end the call. He'd been so distracted by his frustration with Evan that he had forgotten to push that little red button. How could he forget that? How many phone calls had he made from a car before, and how many times had he forgotten to make sure he'd ended a call? Once, twice, ten times, a hundred times? Certainly enough times for it not to be anything new, that's for sure. Yet, there it was. This time the phone call hadn't been ended by Evan, and Tony forgot to press that little red button. Oops.

So, that meant Evan and everyone else in their car heard the conversation between Tony and Gemma. Of course, they *should* have been upstanding citizens and turned off the phone themselves, but what do they say about curiosity? Well, it didn't necessarily kill any cats, but it killed a long-standing relationship stone dead. When they arrived at the hotel, Evan refused to even look at Tony or Gemma. Stony-faced, he dropped off Sharon and the team before getting back into his people carrier and driving away without saying a word.

Confused, Tony asked Sharon where Evan was going. When she told him, it only took a millisecond to shift from confusion to anger. He was absolutely livid. Red-faced and looking like he was about to explode, his first response was: 'How dare Evan leave his phone connected? It was obvious we were having a private conversation!'

These first words out of Tony's lips didn't help calm the shame faced looks of Sharon and the marketing assistants. Instead of making any attempt to contact Evan, Tony chose to ignore him and get on with the evening as planned. When other staff members asked where Evan was, his terse response was that Evan was acting like a child and had 'gone off in a huff'. At some level, Tony must have known that this wasn't going to be helpful, but he was so angry and frustrated by what had happened that he couldn't help himself. He was in a foul mood, and gave his annual 'state of the company' inspirational speech through gritted teeth, all the time silently blaming Evan for ruining the event. At least, he tried to convince himself that it was all Evan's fault, but he knew it wasn't. He knew it was a stupid mistake. While he was sure that Evan should have ended the call as soon as it became clear the conversation was private, Tony also knew that he should have made sure he ended his call to Evan. He couldn't shake the voice in his head that was telling him how stupid he'd been to allow himself to be overheard. He couldn't stop beating himself up, but he wasn't about to admit it – not while he could still be mad at Evan, anyway.

Gemma tried to smooth things over, but that year's dinner and awards was nothing like the evening they had planned and hoped for. She tried all evening to help Tony calm down, but everything she said was just like pouring petrol onto a bonfire; she got singed and the fire raged out of control. The more Tony drank as the evening progressed, the more open he became about his feelings towards Evan. By the time the clock struck midnight, not even Cinderella's fairy godmother could have given the situation a happy ending.

Evan resigned and, shortly afterwards, Sharon did too. Neither wanted to work for a boss who could talk about them in that way – which wasn't really fair or even really true. Their real reason for quitting was that it was less embarrassing than staying. It's easier to play the victim than it is to admit to doing something that brings your integrity into question. Tony and Gemma didn't do anything other than have an honest and frank conversation, albeit about a sensitive issue that wasn't intended to be overheard – whereas Evan and Sharon could never escape from the fact that their integrity was irreversibly compromised. They had to go. There was no way they could stay. Neither could they bring themselves to admit that they were the architects of their own downfall, at fault for choosing to listen to something they were never intended to hear, and then blaming the boss (who, up until then, had been a friend and very supportive towards them). The situation wasn't fair, that's for sure, but it wasn't Evan and Sharon who were the real victims.

That one overheard conversation cost Tony and Gemma a small fortune in time and resources to mend fences with the remaining team. Gossip spread like a bushfire round the company, and was distorted with every re-telling. It didn't matter that the gossip was neither fair nor true; all that mattered was that Tony and Gemma had been embarrassed by a simple mistake. The WTF moment that followed will haunt Tony for years to come. It made him feel sick to the stomach and wasn't easy to forget – but is it something that he could have avoided?

Mistakes will happen and the shit will hit the fan, of that you can be sure, so there's no point in pretending that it won't. It's what you do directly after it happens that counts. Tony's outrage was, on the one hand, understandable, but at the same time was about as useful as a sail on a submarine. He won't be the first person to be caught out that way (to be overheard when they shouldn't have been, to hit 'reply all' when sending a personal email, to text a work colleague with a message that wasn't intended for them saying 'love you', or to inadvertently put kisses at the end of a text or email to their boss). As cringe-worthy as it is to do anything like this, it really isn't an uncommon occurrence. Some people deal with it well; others, not so much.

Tony's anger caused him more problems than the frustration that had caused him to miss ending the call. His anger prevented him from figuring out what he really wanted, not what he thought he had to deal with. He allowed this silly mistake to get in the way of business, cause himself and Gemma an immense amount of heartache, and cost two people their promising careers. That's crazy, over the top, and unnecessary. There were a hundred ways in which Tony could have fixed things. He knows that, I know that, and when you think about it you do too. Intellectually Tony knows he made a mistake. Emotionally, however, he's still mightily upset. No one can blame him for that – but neither does it help resolve anything. Frustration started the ball rolling, and then anger caused the real damage to be done.

Psychology tells us that, when addressing any kind of embarrassment, we should seek clarity quickly. A person who sends a work message with kisses at the end, but then immediately pings back the message: 'Re my last message: as much as I value our relationship, we haven't reached the stage of sending kisses to each other, so please see mine as an intention to build even closer ties ☺' managed to regain control of the situation – and put a smile on the recipient's face to boot. The reason she was able to respond so quickly and so effectively is that she accepted her mistake, took ownership of it, decided what she would like as an outcome, and then did what she could about it. Acceptance, ownership, focusing on outcome, and action are the four essential steps to dealing with embarrassing and potentially damaging situations.

Here's how to avoid doing something that you might regret afterwards:

1 Accept that mistakes are going to happen, and man up when they do. The real regret is not over the initial mistake, but your response when it happens. If you get stuck on the idea that it shouldn't have happened and pretend that embarrassing stuff never happens to anyone, then you will end up regretting the way you behave. A child may stamp their feet and scream the house down because something happens that they can't deal with, but you are not a toddler any more. Behave in that way and you'll look like a child.

2 When something goes wrong, the first thing to consider is not what you wish had happened instead, but what you want to happen now. You must quickly figure out your best-scenario outcome so that you can start putting out the fires you've started with your mistake. The more fires you kill, the less you'll regret making the mistake, and the less damage will be done.

3 If you make a mistake and don't know what to do, do *something* and you will be fine – as long as what you do is positive and takes you closer to fixing things. Trust your instincts: if you feel the need to apologise, then say sorry. If you sense that you've hurt someone's feelings, then ask them if you have. If you need help, then ask for it before it's too late. It doesn't matter how self-reliant or macho you think you are; if you made a mistake then it's your mess to clean up, and if that means seeking support then just do it. People will respect you all the more for keeping your eye on the end goal and not getting caught up with your ego.

15

How to avoid being 'good' but not great

WTF just happened – didn't I do the best I could?

Dean is screwed up because he thinks being good is good enough. For some people, their 'WTF just happened?' moment creeps up on them and then – wham! – reality hits them. Such was the case for Dean. He has developed a face like a smacked backside. To say he looks miserable is an understatement. Looking miserable doesn't begin to describe it. He created a downward spiral of miserableness for himself. This was sad, because it was unnecessary and if he'd confessed sooner that all was not well with him then he could have saved himself a whole heap of miserableness.

Dean's WTF wake-up call happened when he opened his eyes to what was really going on. If you're old enough to remember the TV quiz show *Bullseye* (and if you're not, I'm sure you'll find some clips of it on YouTube), you might remember that the host would rub salt into the emotional wound of the participant who'd failed to win the star prize by saying 'And here's what you could have won!' Dean's WTF moment was a bit like that. In a split second he realised that his 'glass half-full' attitude and belief that being good was good enough was simply wrong. Often, being good just isn't good enough to achieve the things you want. Does that ever happen to you?

That moment when you think you've done enough to earn a reward but then get nothing? I'm afraid it happened to Dean a lot. He thought he was being a good person. He imagined that he always tried to do the right thing – be a good friend, be a good partner, and be a good person. Even so, his so-called friends still moaned about him and he still got dumped by girlfriends, which is sad because, as I said, Dean could have avoided it if only he'd realised the truth – that being 'good' is not good enough.

It's a familiar story. Like Dean, every person who's experienced something similar, including you and me, will think they didn't deserve it, but the sad truth is, they did because, unfortunately, 'good' is just never good enough. People like Dean convince themselves that it will be, because they don't think the world expects much of them. But what you get in life is as much about expectation as it is about dealing with the hand fate has dealt you. Expect a lot from yourself and you'll push yourself to do more; don't expect so much, and that's precisely what you'll get. Dean led himself to believe that he shouldn't expect much from himself because he wasn't worthy of it. It's cringe-worthy and, when you look back at it, extremely silly, but a simple fluke of history was all it took to convince him that being good was enough. It was 'enough' because for some reason Dean felt he wasn't worthy of being anything better than 'good enough'.

You see, Dean had been conditioned to believe that, in the great scheme of things, he was pretty unimportant. Who led him to believe that? No one, really – just circumstances. That belief was in his head and it took him until his WTF moment to figure out that the hard-hearted monster who'd condemned him to a life of 'meh' was none other than himself. How sad is that? He had no one else to blame. His parents didn't abuse him or anything horrid like that; his classmates didn't bully him either; but a chance event led him to form an unhelpful belief himself, and once formed the belief just grew stronger and stronger. All this happened because Dean was born on 22nd November 1963. Now, that date might not mean much to you if you were born outside the United States, but it was the day that President John F. Kennedy was assassinated. That meant for his whole life Dean had had to contend with every birthday being the anniversary of the death of an American legend. Almost as soon as people tired of counting the years, they used the date as an excuse to crank out their own conspiracy theory about the shooting. JFK was like a huge cloud that appeared on Dean's birthday, casting a dark shadow over what should have been the highlight of Dean's year.

It's therefore no surprise that soon Dean didn't look forward to his birthday like other kids. He was soon fed up of not being the centre of attention on the one day of the year when he should be. Instead people said things like:

'Happy birthday, Dean, you know I always remember where I was on the day you were born ...'

or

'Happy birthday, Dean – or should we say isn't this the day JFK was shot?'

It was all pretty lame, especially when Dean heard it year after year. He imagined other people feeling special on their birthday, and deserving to feel special because it was *their* birthday. He didn't feel special, so it followed that he didn't deserve to feel special, and if you are not special there's no need to try to be special, no need to push yourself, and no need to expect more of yourself. Dean simply accepted that as long as he was good, that was good enough.

It should therefore come as no surprise that Dean didn't look forward to his birthday. In fact, Dean didn't look forward to very much at all. Can you blame him? Whatever he did, he made sure it was good enough to get by – he didn't smile unless he had to, didn't laugh unless it was absolutely required, didn't go the extra mile when covering the basics would do, and when his bosses tried to do right by him, he didn't pay any attention to people who urged him to reach his potential. Years later, when people called Dean 'dour' and 'miserable', they were accurate, though unkind. He thought he was just trying to do the right thing, and he imagined that this was necessary to be liked. Unfortunately, when the desire to be liked is perverted into a willingness to be someone else's emotional, and sometimes physical, punch-bag, trouble won't be far behind. This is what happened to Dean.

Dean got married before he was twenty. His wife didn't treat him well. Instead of trying to help her be happy, Dean sucked her into his own misery. Every time they argued, he gave in; every time she yelled at him, he found a reason to justify it; every time it got bad, he allowed it to get worse. He just did the minimum required and hoped it would get better, and of course it didn't. Then the day came when his 'good enough' was no longer good enough for her; she'd had enough, and so left him. For the longest time, Dean couldn't shake the feeling that it must be his fault, but then got over it by telling himself he had been a good husband. He told himself there was nothing more he could have done. She walked out and emptied their joint account, leaving him to figure out how to run a home and care for their two children without her.

No offence, Dean, but come on – you experienced nothing but being beaten up mentally and physically for a decade. She's left you with two young kids and not a penny to your name. You just happened to be born on an unfortunate date. Guess what, your parents didn't mean it; they didn't do it on purpose. Get a grip, Dean – it really wasn't that important, was it? You had birthday parties with loving parents; you weren't in a bombed-out village somewhere searching for scraps of food. You had cake, for goodness' sake!

Clearly Dean did not get it. He didn't realise that he had a choice about what meaning to give to the way he felt. Instead he carried on responding like a five-year-old who's lost his lollipop. Let's face it, in the grand scheme of things, Dean had no reason to mess up his life because of something as silly as his birthday. Yet, here's the thing: Dean isn't the only person reading this who has allowed something in their life to get way out of proportion, is he? It's easy, as an outsider, to ridicule poor old Dean and think that he should get a life, or be grateful for what he's got. However, it might be that something a little closer to home (which to someone else would be as trivial as Dean's birthday) is not so trivial to you. So please be careful about judging Dean. He felt that his experience was horrible and unfair, and yet Dean survived. Not only did he survive, but he got really good at being a martyr. Like a stuck record, he just kept on doing the same thing over and over and over again. He made doormats look bad! He was stuck believing that his version of 'good' was all there was.

Then at last it happened. He woke up on his fiftieth birthday and for some reason the penny finally dropped – being good was never going to be good enough. Doing a good job meant only doing the minimum required to get by and not get fired, and that's exactly how he had been living his life. He did the minimum in his career, the minimum to hang on to his marriage, the minimum to find a new wife and, if he wasn't careful, he would end up doing the minimum as a father. His two children were now teenagers, and needed him to be more than 'good'. It was probably having them around that pushed the button on his milestone birthday and nudged him into a state of clarity. He pledged that, from now on, 'good' would be his minimum standard and not his limit. The truth was, he may not be able to fix the past, but he sure as heck could shape his future. Unusually for Dean, he smiled, because that *is* something to smile about. Hallelujah! Having realised that being good was not good enough, and that he might just have it in him to be great at least some of the time, he learned to ask himself what he really wanted rather than just accepting that what he got was all there was. He learned that, no matter who else was born on his birthday, or who happened to have been shot on it, it was still his birthday.

> ... from now on, 'good' would be his minimum standard and not his limit.

Dean had a wonderful present for his birthday that year. It really doesn't matter that he gave it to himself, because it helped him feel good. Who knows, if Dean keeps on smiling like he is now, then soon somebody else want to help him be even happier. Let's face it, Dean is still not making the most of his life, but it doesn't mean it always has to be this way – for him or for anyone else harbouring a self-inflicted hurt that doesn't need to hurt at all.

Sometimes a WTF moment takes a while to happen. Sometimes the road needs to be well travelled. In Dean's case, it took fifty years of travelling down his road before the penny dropped: happiness doesn't come from just giving – giving in, giving out or giving up. Giving is good when it is in service of the 'greater good', but that's it. Giving for its own sake when it damages the giver is not good.

Psychologists tell us that everyone wants to feel wanted and wants to feel special. They also point out that everyone constructs their own mental 'filter' that matches patterns that already exist in the brain to new experiences. Dean's filter made any possibility of being 'second best' or 'not good enough' appear as if by magic! The same events seen through other eyes would have been interpreted differently, but Dean's filter always found a reason for him to be miserable. Dean accidentally learned to feel unwanted. There's no way Dean could change what had happened, but he could make darn sure that from now on he'd ask better questions of himself to try to see things differently.

Dean could have asked himself a better question, but he didn't. There was no need for him to be a martyr. Feeling special comes naturally when you're helping someone else to feel special too, not by being a doormat. The penny finally dropped: doing the right thing wasn't the same as seeking approval. He learned that allowing people to walk all over him not only made him feel bad, but ended up making whoever was doing the walking feel pretty horrid as well. It may have taken fifty years, but at last he had learned.

Now try asking yourself these questions, to help you avoid doing the wrong thing:

2. Ask yourself, am I using my strengths to make myself happy and raise my standards beyond being merely good? If I choose to believe that I can be great at certain aspects of my life, what can I do to start on that path? And if 'great' were to become my personal standard for everything in life, how different would my life be?

1. How special do you feel? Be careful how you think about this: feeling special for a crappy reason isn't really feeling special at all. 'I'm special because no one could be as stupid as I am' is, first, probably not true (you've no idea how many really stupid people there are out there). Second, that's not what I mean by special. I mean special in the 'Wow, I'm actually amazing and wonderful in my own quirky way' sort of special, not any other kind. So be careful.

3. Make sure you know that something about you is special. Now you know, ask yourself, what am I doing that helps other people feel special too? What's the best way to feel good about doing the right thing and remaining special? How do I incorporate helping others to feel special, doing the right thing, and making sure I stay special too, into my everyday activities?

How to avoid getting fired

WTF just happened to my job?

After years of working for the same company, and being successful, out of the blue Helen was sacked. She was mourned for a moment, but then forgotten within a couple of days. So much for loyalty, eh?

Here's the thing about having a job: feelings of certainty and confidence are terrific, particularly when they're nicely balanced with feelings of stimulation and excitement. Think about it as if you were a Formula One driver: the balance of knowing you can do something and yet still feeling challenged by doing it is as good for you as it is for that driver when he's feeling confident about his ability and he's excited about the thrill of a race he believes he can win. However, there is a difference in the world of work. The driver has his hands on the wheel and he – and only he – can turn it. He doesn't control the other people in the race – which is why only one person can win, and why not everyone survives. Helen found out that, in the workplace, feelings of control and certainty are an illusion – and so was imagining that she could control the risk that goes with the job. You can control your loyalty, but you can't control anyone else's loyalty to you.

Company loyalty may be overrated. Too much work makes Helen a dull girl, and too much belief in an employer's loyalty makes Helen a dumb girl. Of course, it's a good thing to have mutual trust and confidence in your boss and your company, but if you lose sight of reality, it can end up biting you somewhere painful. Then when it catches you by surprise it's all the more painful. It hurts. Not only because your ego has just been stomped on, but also because it feels a lot like being jilted. In your head you know it's just about a job and probably isn't personal, but emotionally you feel rejected, as if someone has stabbed you through the heart. It really hurts.

Helen loved her job and her employer. She's not prone to outward shows of affection, so didn't go around making a big deal of it. But anyone who knew her would say, 'If you cut Helen in two, she'd have the company logo running through her.' She was also good at her job. Starting as a junior manager, she'd risen through the ranks to become head of her division, won awards for business performance, and was loved by her team.

They say that you're only two pay cheques away from being on the street. Not that Helen's employer actually wanted to put her out on the street, it's just that they didn't think twice about making the decision to let an employee go if the business circumstances demanded it. The prevailing culture was that loyalty to the business objectives was stronger than loyalty to any particular individual. They moved her to a new division – one that was performing poorly. They told her everyone had confidence in her. They told her she had their full support. Then when the market could not support improvements, no matter what she did, they sent someone to fire her. To add insult to injury, Helen had been a mentor to this woman. There was no discussion, no second chances, just a short and to-the-point letter.

Fifteen years' service was brought to an abrupt end after a fifteen-minute conversation. Helen was handed a cheque (to avoid legal proceedings) and asked to leave. She was history, and you can be reasonably sure that at the same time as she was being let go, to save face for someone higher up the food chain, some woman fifteen years her junior was being welcomed into the corporate 'family'. It's also reasonable to predict that history repeats itself. Maybe job offers should carry a warning: 'Not all promises may be honoured – employees planning a future at this company do so at their own risk.'

The lesson here? Don't be dull, but more importantly don't be dumb. *You* are the only person you can ultimately rely on to provide for yourself and your family. Taking a job is doing a deal. You put your working life at the disposal of an employer, and they agree to pay you. Even the peripherals – like holiday pay, insurance and pensions – are just part of that pay. They hire you; they don't marry you, they don't own you – and you certainly don't own them. It's just a deal. No more and no less. If you are dumb enough to confuse self-interest for genuine commitment, then more fool you. They may like you, but they don't love you. They may care about you but they don't care *for* you. They are your employers, not your life partners.

Psychologists say that humans struggle to separate feelings based on work and non-work life. They say that the brain can't differentiate between feelings based on where they occurred, only by what they are. In practice, that means that if you like chocolate cake your brain creates the chemistry that might make you smile as the chocolate cake is delivered to your table in real life. It will cause you to have very similar feelings when you later remember eating that chocolate cake. The cake is gone and you are no longer in the restaurant, but the good feeling may still be as strong. Similarly, something may happen to you at work and cause you to express an emotion. Later, you may think about that event at home and still feel the same emotion. You didn't have to be at work to feel what it was like to be there. In fact, it's more – not less – likely that feelings are heightened at work than at home. That's because we are more alert to self-protection at work. There's more to threaten us, so we are more prone to being subconsciously aware of threats. You may have noticed that people have a habit of starting new relationships in the workplace, even when they're in a relationship already. It happens because it's so easy to confuse heightened emotions with real feelings. Not that feelings in a work relationship can't be real – it's just that most of the heavy breathing in broom closets doesn't happen because fate brought people together. Unfortunately, that means we fall for the company just as easily, and end up emotionally investing in it just as readily.

The good news is that, when you see things as they are, rather than through rose-coloured spectacles, you can have a great relationship with your employer – and you can deal with changes to the original deal as they happen. If Helen hadn't been sucked into a false sense of security, she could have handled herself much better. The false belief was no one's doing but her own; the company never claimed any relationship with her other than being her employer. The change happened in her own head without her ever being consciously aware of it, so she had a good excuse. You, on the other hand, are reading this and have no excuse. You can't go blaming a big, uncaring conglomerate for firing you when the economy makes you too expensive to keep on the payroll. Instead, you can start asking better questions before that happens.

No one knows how safe your job is better than you do. Things are either going well – or they're not. Business is good – or it's not. You are adding more than enough value to secure your place – or you're not. And if you don't know, then you don't deserve to be there anyway. Whatever. Your future is in your own hands, not anyone else's. If you are offered a new role, think of it as a renegotiation of your original deal. If it's a kamikaze mission, then figure out a deal that works before you accept it. If it's a risk, then balance that risk. If it's something you can't avoid, and you fear the worst, then start making other plans. When you quit, your employer won't be half as upset as you will be if they later choose to let you go.

Psychology teaches us that human beings really don't know what's going on in the world; they only ever know what's going on in their world, in their field of vision, and in their interpretation of events. People put frames around reality, much as an artist puts a frame around a picture, or a window frames the scenery outside. Move the window and the scenery changes. Put the picture into a smaller frame, and what's not seen any more gets lost. It's all too easy to forget that the world you are experiencing isn't all there is: the company you work for isn't the only company there is, the people you think you know have lives outside your field of vision, and the constructs you've made about the future are no more reliable than a dream.

There are no easy answers to difficult situations, but if you recognise the brutal reality of the working world, then when the worst happens it'll feel a heck of a lot less brutal. When you're prepared, you're rarely caught by surprise.

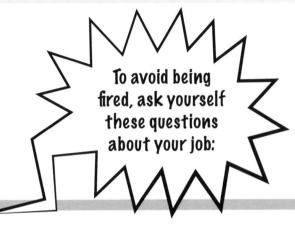

To avoid being fired, ask yourself these questions about your job:

1   When did you last review the deal you have with your employers? This is not an excuse to demand or beg for a pay rise. That may end up getting you fired anyway, so it's not a great idea. It's a question that makes you re-evaluate whether you are actually doing what you are being paid to do. Helen wasn't treated fairly, but not all 'WTF, I just got fired' moments are unfair. There are plenty of employees who get sloppy and take things for granted. They may have appreciated the wonderful benefits and great bonuses when they got the job. They may even work hard and do a great job ... for a while. They may also forget all about that after a few years of being with the company and comparing themselves to people they perceive as being 'worse' than they are. This false sense of security and unappreciative attitude won't go unnoticed. Then, one day, when it's least expected, the WTF moment will happen — and it'll be no one's fault but their own.

2   How much value are you really adding? You may not be married to the firm, but you do have a symbiotic relationship with it. Your company can't function without you ~ at least, until they replace you or get another employee to cover your work. You can't function without them, unless someone else is paying you and giving you opportunities to advance your career. That means you must ensure they want you, and the best way to do that is to give them what they are paying you for … and just a little bit more. The chances are that simply being more aware of what you are doing to add value will help you add even more.

3   How might you add even more value, and add to your own value simultaneously? This does mean eventually asking for more money, more responsibility, more *something*. However, you should only do this at the appropriate time and in the appropriate place. If you don't have performance appraisals with your boss, then arrange one. If your performance reviews are appraisals, then get that bit over with before talking about the future and all the value you want to add. If you don't have a plan for yourself, then you can be pretty sure that someone else will. I don't know about you, but I'd rather be monitoring how I'm doing on my own plan than trying to figure out how I'm fitting into someone else's plan.

How to avoid unpleasant romantic 'surprises'

WTF just happened to my love life?

Bev wasn't jilted at the altar. It was much worse than that. Really - much, much worse! You see, Bev thought she knew what was going on in her personal life because she'd told herself so, over and over. The trouble is, people lie. They not only fail to tell the truth, but they often purposely deceive, have their own agendas, and can be thoroughly untrustworthy - and those are just the people who tell you they love you! Or, at least that's what happened to Bev. And if experience is anything to go by, then Bev isn't alone. Even if her particular story is a little unusual, the practice of duping yourself by making stuff up and then pretending it's real certainly isn't.

If you actually believed Boy George in the 1980s when he famously said he would rather have a cup of tea than sex, then you've either had, or are going to have, one of these WTF moments. He may well have enjoyed a nice cuppa but, like any young man with a libido, he probably liked other activities too, some of which are best kept private. Today, of course, in this world of instant messaging and an ever-present paparazzi armed with mobile phones ready to send an incriminating picture around the globe in seconds, it's very hard to keep a secret. Unfortunately, most people don't see themselves as celebrities. Perhaps they should.

Then again, there's Bev. Bev was almost a celebrity – that may be a bit of a stretch, but in her mind she was already more famous than most. As a research scientist, most of the things she did at work went over the heads of everyday folk, but Bev was smart in more ways than just being science-smart. She knew how to talk about her smart stuff in ways that most of us can understand. Far from being bored, people found what she had to say really interesting. Bev had discovered a way of making unfathomable scientific information not just accessible, but really fun and interesting to read. Bev also had a wonderfully deep resonant voice that made her podcasts and videos hugely successful. From a successful blog, she'd progressed to writing articles then, not long after that, bestselling books.

Everything seemed to be going brilliantly for Bev. Still only in her thirties, physically attractive, and über-smart, with a classy accent, it looked as if she would soon be snapped up. He had popped the question, she had said yes, and production companies were sniffing round her like customs dogs at Glastonbury. So it looked very much like she'd soon be on TV. At least, it wouldn't have been long if she hadn't had her WTF moment the week before her planned trip down the aisle. There's every chance she would have been a household name already – or at the very least been invited on a daytime celebrity game show. She's not – not because she shouldn't be, but because now she's not ready to be. She's not ready because she had an unpleasant surprise: a WTF moment. She, like so many people, experienced a problem in one part of her life that affected the other. In her case the problem was with her upcoming nuptials.

Bev wasn't jilted or left standing at the altar, nor did an old boyfriend turn up yelling 'it should have been me'. Her WTF moment need not have been a surprise, and that makes it a whole lot worse. Bev had known Graham since high school and, if she had paid attention, would have realised that Graham's orientation was not the same as hers. They hadn't dated back then, but shared some interests and had been good friends, and if they had stayed that way it would have ended better for both of them. Graham went off to Warwick while Bev went up to Cambridge as an undergraduate, and then to complete her master's and PhD.

They are both smart but Graham's rise in academia had not been quite as fast as Bev's. He'd stepped out of the world of research into a lucrative job with a corporate giant and had lived in the United States for close to ten years. Eventually he returned to London with a West Coast tan and a slight accent. His well-paid job allowed him anonymity which suited him, and his workmates knew little about his life outside the office. He was 'tall Graham, the quiet bloke from head office who does triathlons and has a funny accent'. They had no idea that Graham was a gay man, conflicted about his identity and confused about his relationship with Bev, who he had met again by chance at a corporate shindig in Las Vegas. It was more destination than destiny as they just happened to be in the same place at the same time. Graham had caught her eye by being the only man not dressed in a boring grey suit and dark tie. They met for a drink and as one glass led to another, then to dinner, Bev might have been ready for more. Nothing happened as Graham was a complete gentleman. He said goodnight outside her room, despite her suggestion to raid the mini-bar.

After a fortnight of not hearing from Graham she assumed her impression of 'chemistry' might have only been a Bacchus blessing and so set any thoughts of romance aside. Then just as the memory was fading, he called. It was another dinner invitation. This time he was entertaining a business client and his wife and hoped that Bev would be his date to make up a foursome. She accepted and so began a slow but steady courtship over the next three years. Yes, you read that correctly – three years. And, no, this was not the 1940s! She later recollected that she was hardly swept off her feet, but their relationship was pleasant all the same. Graham was a very nice man, physically fit, and definitely smart enough to keep up with her. He was financially stable, didn't take drugs or binge on alcohol, didn't have an ex-wife and a brood of dependent children, so what was there not to like? Later she speculated that she might have 'known' on some level that Graham was gay but didn't want to raise the subject with him because she liked the relationship, and she really liked Graham. Like turned to conversations of a deeper relationship, then eventually Graham proposed and they set a date. Theirs wasn't a traditional Mills & Boon love affair, but Bev hadn't journeyed down this road before so didn't have anything to compare it with.

You've probably guessed that they didn't rush into marriage. After all, they hadn't rushed so far, so why start now? They had a little over a year to make the necessary arrangements. Planning weddings wasn't really Bev's thing – she wasn't even all that fussed about the white dress. When Graham arranged for samples of various flowers to be delivered, along with choices of ribbon for the invites and menus, she wasn't put out in the slightest; in fact, he was so brilliant that if he hadn't already been good at his job he could have jacked it in and become a wedding planner. Perhaps if you knew that, after nearly four years of 'courting', they hadn't actually done the deed yet it starts to get a little clearer. As obviously stereotypical as this all sounds, of course I don't mean to suggest that every fit man who is bright, bubbly and interested in fashion, likes planning a wedding and is prepared to wait until the wedding night to have sex is gay. But the fact is that Graham was. So when Bev unexpectedly arrived at the hotel to check a few final details and found Graham testing out the bed in the bridal suite with a very male, very gay florist, her latent suspicions were vividly confirmed. Having never met Graham I can only speculate on the conflict and confusion that he was likely to have been going through. It can't have been easy on either of them.

If ever there was a WTF moment, this was it. They say that your life story plays out in front of you just before you die. For Bev, the history of every 'clue' played out in front of her from their very first meeting; she realised that, at some level, she had always known, but for some reason she had never addressed the elephant in the room. If only she had. If only she had simply asked a few better questions, it all could have been avoided. If she had quit believing her own mental version of events and looked hard at the reality of the evidence in front of her, then surely she would have had better questions to ask, because the story she believed in was not the story being played out in the real world.

Psychologists tell us that there are two aspects to falling in love and staying in love. The first is straightforward sexual chemistry: sparks fly when two people are attracted to each other. The second aspect is compatibility: when sparks are flying, a man produces more oestrogen than normal so will appear concerned with being caring and making a nest, whereas a woman produces more testosterone and so appears more concerned with having sex whenever and wherever the opportunity arises. However, this soon wears off and the need for compatibility replaces it. Couples need to have something to feel compatible over: this might mean sharing values, sharing interests, or sharing the fact that your interests are so wildly different that you want to explore each other's. For love to last, both chemistry and compatibility are required.

Here's how to avoid doing something that you might regret afterwards:

1   When in doubt, say what's on your mind. If you ask a question with the express intent of gaining clarity, then, sure as eggs are eggs, you'll unscramble any confusion. It may not be easy or comfortable, but the alternative — bottling it up — can only end badly.

2   When you have a doubt about something, then look for alternatives before
    accepting anything at face value. Your gut feeling is a part of your brain trying
    to tell you something; you can't know whether that feeling is telling you that what
    you are doing is right, or if it's telling you to get the heck out of there because
    what you are doing is wrong. All you can deduce is that there is 'something' for
    you to investigate, and it is up to you to figure out what it is and if it is important.
    Chances are, any worries you have come from the latent suspicion caused by
    binge-watching crime drama on Netflix, but it's better to probe and be wrong than
    hear that little voice in your head say 'I told you so.'

3   When you eat the first thing you see without looking at a menu, then you shouldn't
    be surprised when it's not to your taste. Like a restaurant is full of different
    dishes, some of which will be to your taste and some that won't be, so the world
    is full of potential matches, some of which will be a good fit and some not so
    much. Imagine how disappointed you'd be if you went to the restaurant convinced
    that you only have one shot at ordering a meal you'll love, and then when the
    food came it wasn't all that. How easy would it be to convince yourself to make
    do, because there might not be another meal choice after this one? I'm not
    suggesting you need to eat your way through the whole menu, but you do have to
    open your eyes to the choice. The same is true for finding love. Who knows, you
    may well be 'fated' to meet the love of your life, but it doesn't hurt to double-check
    before jumping in with both feet. Be sure to try before you buy, and never be
    afraid to take a chance, either to wait for the 'right one' or, if it feels like it is right,
    to take the risk. If you have thought things through then it's probably going to be
    worth it.

How to avoid your darling children turning into teenage monsters

WTF just happened to my little angels?

Everyone says their kids can be a nightmare, but Karen and Michael's kids proved it. If you've ever had to smile through gritted teeth and listen to yet another doting parent tell you how brilliant their little one is, then you'll know how irritating that can be. Better still, if you've found yourself secretly chuckling about the fact that a friend's pride and joy is about to be expelled for dealing weed, or a friend's child with an expensive degree has just got a job stacking shelves in a supermarket, then you already know that not every child turns out as their parents hoped they would. By the way, none of the above predicts how well the kid will do in life: some of the most successful people I know have done— Discretion prevents me from saying more, but you get the idea. But Karen and Michael didn't 'get it'; they didn't get it at all.

Nature can be troublesome. One day your child can't wait to hold Mum or Dad's hand wherever you are, then something happens and suddenly they don't want to be seen near you, never mind touching you. Adoring glances have become shifty looks, and straight answers to simple questions are a thing of the past. Then there's that moment when some clever dick chuckles at your discomfort and patronisingly assures you that it will pass ... Be assured you are not alone in wanting to punch them. Knowing that it will pass and waiting for it to pass are not the same.

Karen and Michael both had children from a previous relationship when they met, and both had previous partners who had raised them. Karen had travelled so much with her job that her ex-husband, and then his new wife, had done the bulk of the parenting, leaving Karen with occasional visits. At first this had included holidays, but as the children grew and became more independent, contact grew more infrequent. Karen was busy with her life and convinced herself that her kids were better off as they were, so had no idea what the transition from childhood to adolescence was really like. Michael's story was similar, apart from the fact that his ex-wife had fought tooth and nail to keep him away from her children and her new family. The result was the same: infrequent contact, superficial relationships, and no clue what would happened to their children when their growth hormones started to kick in. This was unfortunate in many ways, but in particular because of the false sense of security Karen and Michael had. They had decided to have children together, and imagined that because they were already parents to almost grown-up children that they knew how to parent. They didn't. In their late forties, they were no more equipped to deal with the transition from angel to monster than any other couple left wondering WTF just happened?

Another difference for Karmichael (yes, I know it's corny, but they were from the *Friends* era, and so imagined that linking their names together was cute). The difference between Karmichael and a young couple doing it all for the first time was that they honestly believed that both they and their darling offspring were special. You may have noticed that this appears to be the rule with older parents, particularly with a second set of offspring. Scott and Eva, born just a year apart almost to the day, were no exception to that rule.

'You could tell he was going to be gifted when he was a baby,' cooed Karen.

'And he's head and shoulders above his classmates. If we lived in the States they would definitely have him skip a couple of grades,' Michael would chip in.

The fact that his primary school teachers described Scott as just a normal, bright young boy didn't feature in their ego-driven fantasy. Eva, of course, was enrolled in every 'girlie' after-school activity possible. The nanny was kept busy taking her to ballet, drama, riding, piano and violin lessons, and Scott went to plenty of 'boy' after-school sporty activities. This had the benefit of giving Karmichael tons of boasting material (as well as being an excuse to only actually see their kids at bedtime and just before school). However, Scott did not manifest his genius and figure out a new unified theory before his thirteenth birthday. Eva did not become a debutante and marry into royalty. Karmichael didn't actually own up to hoping that she would, but everyone knew that's what they were secretly hoping. Things did not turn out anything like that.

The school had arranged for the boys first rugby team to go on a six-week rugby tour to South Africa. For months beforehand, Scott had been increasingly withdrawn and sullen. Karmichael put it down to nerves about being away from home for so long, and were forgiving. His sister rolled her eyes whenever Karen or Michael tried to say anything vaguely reassuring, and just gave them a knowing stare – the one that said 'For God's sake, don't you know anything?' but it went right over both their heads.

> Karen now either avoided mentioning her children to her friends at all, or simply described them as 'going through a difficult phase'.

Neither was Eva meeting parental expectations. Now she was sixteen, Karen had even offered to buy tickets to Glastonbury and go with her and a group of her friends. Being told that she had 'no idea' simply left her confused. Karen now either avoided mentioning her children to her friends at all, or simply described them as 'going through a difficult phase'.

The call from South Africa left them stunned. Michael drove to Heathrow to pick up Scott. After collecting him from a member of the airline staff and getting Scott into the car he demanded an explanation. All he got was a shrug of the shoulders and a grunt.

'What possessed you to go out on your own, and why do they think you were trying to buy drugs?'

More shrugging.

'We are not leaving here until I get an explanation!'

'Stuff you!' was Scott's reply, and with that he tried to open the car door and escape. Angry beyond measure and pumped with adrenaline, Michael reached over and closed the door, cracking his elbow into Scott's nose and pushing him hard back into the car seat. Much screaming and shouting ensued, with plenty of inventive language from young Scott. Within a few minutes, the car had been approached by armed police officers; they were in a car park at Heathrow Airport, after all. Michael was arrested and Scott restrained while still screaming abuse, the blood from his broken nose backing up his story that Michael had attacked him.

Michael was charged with causing actual bodily harm, even though he protested his innocence, and when the drugs situation was investigated they discovered that the nanny had been Scott's supplier of illegal substances. Scott was taken from his parents while the courts investigated his father, and the nanny was prosecuted and is now in prison. Then Eva confessed to knowing about the drugs from the start and for despising Karmichael for being full of their own self-importance and being rotten parents. It pushed Karen close to the edge. When Eva then announced that she was a lesbian, this tipped Karen over the edge. Karen blamed Michael, and Michael had no idea what had happened to the confident, self-assured woman he had married. Karmichael was no more. Whatever they'd once felt for each other had turned sour, and they are now divorced. The good news is that most of Scott's next year was spent in rehab rather than in care or prison. Not only did he survive, but it must have acted as a wake-up call. He turned his life around and has just completed a degree. Eva, meanwhile, soon discovered that living with a girlfriend wasn't working for her. She couldn't help the fact that she actually liked boys and was more attracted to being straight than she was to trying to antagonise her parents. Now she is also in further education and has a boyfriend. Eva doesn't dance, act or ride ponies, but will admit that learning how to do all those things wasn't a bad thing to have done after all. She still plays the piano and violin and loves them, particularly as she met her boyfriend through playing music.

Karen has become a 'serial enthusiast', but doesn't actually *do* anything. One day she is enthusiastic about becoming this and then a week later about that. Under all that enthusiasm she is miserable. She admits to her therapist that she cries herself to sleep and demands more and more pills from her doctor to help. They won't help to fix anything, but may dull the pain.

Michael is angry. He is angry that his reputation was sullied. He is angry because his wife didn't support him. He is angry that his children were so disrespectful. He is angry that the nanny he trusted (ironically, as he was having an affair with her) was taking her pay, the additional under the table cash he gave her, and Scott's allowance, and making more money than he did by supplying some of the neighbourhood kids with drugs. Most of all, he was angry because, deep down, he knew it was all his own fault; he knew that it was up to him to be a proper father, and that having abdicated that responsibility once already, this had been his chance to redeem himself, but he hadn't. In the end, the only person he could be angry with was himself, and for that there appeared no remedy or release.

> They are now the first to admit that being a good parent is measured by the safety and well-being of their children.

It was too late for Karen and Michael to recognise that being a successful parent is not measured by how much they pay in school fees, how well their children's school does in the annual rankings, how often their kids are chosen for this honour or that, or by how much their child is an extension of their own ego. They are now the first to admit that being a good parent is measured by the safety and well-being of their children. They now know that kids don't care about material things when they feel secure in a strong family unit, are excited by being part of their family, feel valued because of who they are, not what they achieve, and – most of all – when they genuinely feel unconditionally loved.

Psychology reveals that all human beings have basic driving needs and will find ways of meeting those needs merely to survive. Everyone needs to feel in control and certain of themselves; if children don't find that at home, then they will find it somewhere or in something else. As well as feeling in control, we all need to feel a bit of risk and excitement to keep that control from being boring; children who don't find excitement in a positive way will get it elsewhere. Everyone needs to feel special and that they belong. Feeling special is the opposite of having to prove yourself: if a child feels the need to constantly perform, then they will decide they are special in a different, less positive way. Genuine feelings of belonging come from unconditional love: a child who feels their only way to gain approval is by achieving something - being top in their class, picked for the top football team, being the best at something - will seek out people who approve of them unconditionally. Unfortunately, that's almost always a bad thing because they mistake feeling 'significant' with feeling loved. They can be significant by being special in a bad way, but that's far less likely to happen when they feel special because they know they are loved.

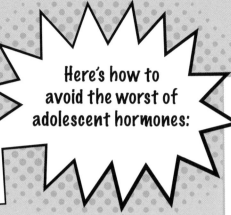

Here's how to avoid the worst of adolescent hormones:

1 If you treat children like a borrowed item that has to be tended to and one day given back, then you might avoid making parenting all about you. It's all about focus. If a person is focused on outcome, then it's less likely they'll get caught up with irrelevant issues. Boasting about a kid's brilliance is an 'issue'. Helping a kid become brilliant is an 'outcome'.

2 If you are honest, there's only one person you can't lie to – yourself. Even if it takes a while to recognise it, we all know that feeling we get when something just doesn't feel right. That's the feeling you should be looking for when it comes to raising offspring. It's not a problem if you feel it and then do something to (a) recognise what's causing it, and then (b) fix it. It is a problem if you ignore it.

3 If you are true to yourself, then you are likely to be true to your children. Have you asked yourself the tough questions about what you want for yourself out of life, and what you want for them? If not, what's stopping you? The clearer you are about what you want, the more likely it is that you can figure out what to do about it.

How to avoid letting yourself go

WTF just happened to the style I was so proud of?

Christine got stuck in a time warp: that can happen when you take your eye off the ball. The minute you let your standards drop, then *boom*: bad stuff happens - you pay less attention, you let things slide, and you wake up one day wondering 'WTF just happened?' Time can catch you unawares; one day you're young and sexy, and then the years speed up. Trust me, if you haven't experienced it yet then you will, because time really does feel like it passes faster the older you get. I'm not talking about getting all grey and wrinkly; it can happen before you realise it. Unlike lots of the stories in here, however, I'm afraid there is no fix for time. I don't have a magic wand to turn back the clock, but instead of following Christine's example, you can surf on top of the waves of time rather than have them crash over you.

Personal dress standards can drop faster than Speedos on a naturist beach. It can happen to anyone. It seems to happen every year; one minute you see someone dancing athletically on a music channel, and within months something happens and they've gone from sex kitten to chubby cat whose only way back into the limelight is with an exercise and diet DVD. Change happens quickly. Hold up a mirror to yourself: not only will you see what you really look like, but you'll see what you're doing to make yourself look that way. If you want to change the way you look, then you'd better change the things you do. Style is not just something that young people have. In fact, most young people don't have style; they have attitude, and that's not the same. Everyone wants to feel special. Some people feel special by making a point of telling everyone they don't need to feel special – because of course that makes them feel ... special. Other people, particularly young people, think being special comes from adopting their own style. Often, their style is the same as their friends' style (they all have tattoos, they all pierce unmentionable body parts and wear clothes from the same high street brands), which means that they are all uniquely similar rather than being actually unique.

Christine had been one of those girls when she'd been that age. In her day there had been no eBay or cheap clothing shops; clothes were still made to last and internet auction sites had yet to be invented. Living and working in London, she'd styled herself on the It girls of the time, buying knock-off versions of designer gear in street markets, and styling her hair to match whatever looked trendy – and whatever her mates were doing. This was the mid-1980s, and at twenty Christine saw herself as a girl of her time. Barry Manilow might not have written 'Copacabana' about Christine, but she had certainly got caught in a time warp of her own making. She was an ordinary girl, doing an ordinary job, earning ordinary wages – but in an environment where nobody wanted to be seen as ordinary.

Christine's path to letting herself go was far more gradual and much less glamorous than Barry Manilow's 'Lola'. The dreams and hopes fuelled by the hype of the day – anyone can have what they want if they just go for it – might have been widely believed, but didn't work for her. Her parents' post-Second World War generation may have been the baby boomers, grateful to live without rationing and being bombed, but hers was post-flower power, post-love-ins – and post-gratitude. This was soon to be the world of ordinary people making their fortune and lunch being 'only for wimps'. It was a world of change in which everything was new, exciting and possible: MTV brought the latest pop music and videos into the bedroom of every teenager with a portable TV; it was a world where computers started to be accessible: the Sinclair Spectrum may have been a basic machine, but was widely available and relatively cheap.

Christine didn't question that her life would be glamorous, sexy, fun and special; this was the life she was born into and 'deserved'. As far as Christine was concerned, all she needed to do was turn up to life and it would all happen for her. She fell into a routine that included a Friday ritual at a certain well-known hotel where she and her friends would meet after work to sip champagne and pose. When it began, I suppose, it was quite stylish, but after almost two decades it had become an excuse to start the weekend early with a boozy binge. Perhaps the football-jersey-style T-shirts emblazoned with glitter and sequins had been stylish once. They weren't any more. Christine was a member of the hard core and while other Friday-afternooners had come and gone, she and her three buddies were the Pink Ladies of London's West End hotel scene. Except the real Pink Ladies from *Grease* probably had more style and definitely had more class. More than once, the Friday-afternooners had been asked to leave the hotel bar, and had been lucky that the request hadn't become permanent. The staff and customers in that hotel did not look at Christine and her Friday-afternooners and whisper about how glamorous and stylish they were. They were more likely shaking their heads in disgust at their drunken antics.

However, it wasn't a road to Damascus realisation that caused Christine's 'WTF just happened?' moment. It was meeting Jeff. He'd been standing on the platform at Marylebone, calling her name, and it had taken her a few seconds to recognise him. Jeff looked great. He'd filled out from the skinny intern she'd known years ago, but it really suited him. His suit was clearly tailored and his crisp white shirt set off his natural skin tone. He looked great. The trouble was, the look that Jeff gave her wasn't what she was hoping for. He didn't say anything, but she just knew that the way she looked at him was not the same way he was looking at her. She couldn't help having a glint in her eye and more than a hint of admiration for the way he'd clearly taken care of himself. He, on the other hand, had no such glint or hint for what he was seeing. Call it intuition, body language or unconscious communication, there was no doubt in her mind. In that instant she caught a glimpse of herself and in one gut-wrenching moment realised that she had let herself go. She didn't need him to say anything, not that he was likely to, because her interpretation of his glance was all it took to make her recognise her own reality. That was the moment. That was when she looked at herself and asked, 'WTF happened to me?' She looked down at her clothes. It wasn't Friday, so she wasn't wearing a designer T-shirt, but she was wearing the same style of jacket and skirt she had worn twenty years ago. Her current black skirt and jacket may have cost more than she'd been able to afford back then, but the look was the same. Her hair hadn't needed dying black back then, but it did now.

In a flash she became aware that while the skinny Jeff had blossomed into a sexy mature man, she'd matured more like an old cheese. All she could say to herself was, 'What was I thinking?'

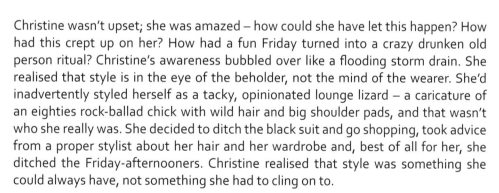

She realised that style is in the eye of the beholder, not the mind of the wearer.

Christine wasn't upset; she was amazed – how could she have let this happen? How had this crept up on her? How had a fun Friday turned into a crazy drunken old person ritual? Christine's awareness bubbled over like a flooding storm drain. She realised that style is in the eye of the beholder, not the mind of the wearer. She'd inadvertently styled herself as a tacky, opinionated lounge lizard – a caricature of an eighties rock-ballad chick with wild hair and big shoulder pads, and that wasn't who she really was. She decided to ditch the black suit and go shopping, took advice from a proper stylist about her hair and her wardrobe and, best of all for her, she ditched the Friday-afternooners. Christine realised that style was something she could always have, not something she had to cling on to.

What a shame it took her so long to figure it out.

The psychology of self-awareness is complicated. Suffice it to say that everyone has blind spots. Some people have dysmorphia: they either see themselves as bigger, taller, fatter, thinner, more handsome, less handsome, more beautiful or uglier than they really are – and the rest of the world tells them they are. They can be told they weigh eight stone and their BMI is too low, but still believe they are fat. They can be shown photographs of themselves alongside other people for comparison and still not see what everyone else can see. Many people have their own misunderstandings about the way other people see them; most people look at themselves face on in the mirror and don't see their profile like other people do; most people style their hair, doing only what they can see, and have no idea what they look like from behind; and today most people take multiple selfies until they're happy with one, which they put on social media. But there are no retakes in real life. What people see for the first time can never be unseen.

Here's how to avoid letting yourself go:

1 Remember that having style is a choice: it's asking yourself 'How do I want to look, and how do I want to behave?' so that you get as close as you can to your ideal. You do style for you, not anyone else, and as long as you know you are doing it for you you'll keep on doing it; do it for someone or something else and why would it last? It's meaningless. Do it for yourself.

2 Remember that time passes even more quickly when we are not paying attention. People let themselves go when they feel comfortable as they are. If you go on holiday for a couple of weeks and stay in one place, time passes quickly as soon as you feel comfortable with where you are, but if you change location two or three times, the holiday will feel like it has lasted way longer ~ because you were paying attention. Pay attention to the effect that time has on you and your style, and you won't let yourself go.

3 Remember to grow, and change, the way you present yourself to the world so that it is consistent with the way you want the world to see you. It's unlikely that you will have the same views, values or priorities, or the same choice of lifestyle at different points in your life. Therefore it is perfectly reasonable for you to reinvent yourself as often as you want to, simply to make the best of who you are at that time. There are people who make their style so consistent that it becomes their identity, and they don't change with fashions or with what's popular at the time. However, those people are rare. For them, they make the best of who they are by being who they are purposefully and with great clarity. As opposed to the person who simply loses an awareness of themselves as they get caught up in life, and who doesn't notice time passing or themselves changing. It's not just about being age-appropriate, or wearing something comfortable, and while this story is about a woman, it applies just as much to men. Being the best you can be and presenting yourself to the world in ways that make the most of yourself is an issue for anyone who wants to avoid a 'WTF just happened to my style?' moment.

How to avoid tying the knot with the wrong person

WTF just happened – how do you know someone is really your soul mate?

True love doesn't let anything get in the way. Just ask Jenni and Albert, because they didn't let little things like continents, laws or negative beliefs stand in their way. You see, not by any means are all WTF moments gut-churning, heart-stopping horrid moments. Sometimes (perhaps only on very few occasions, but still sometimes) the world taps you on the shoulder and, yes, your heart stops, and, yes, your gut churns, but this time for something good and special. Lasting relationships need two things: chemistry and compatibility. Both are necessary. Run out of chemistry, and it's just a waiting game to discover which one of you bails first. Realise too late that you're not actually compatible, and one or both of you will end up despising the other. Finding a soul mate takes way more than a 'match' online. The last time I looked there were simple rules of engagement for when people fancy each other. If they are both up for it, then it's hard to hide. Eyes connecting, sly smiles, surreptitious touching – it'll all be there. Here's the thing: it won't matter to him that the soles of her shoes are red or the bag she carries has a big gold medallion, and she really won't notice the label inside his suit or the logo on his wristwatch - at least, not in any way that affects whether they fancy each other or not. They either will or they won't. Then, when it gets serious, it'll only work if they like each other after the frantic sex has cooled, for cool it surely will.

Albert was just nineteen when he had his 'WTF just happened?' moment. He was supposed to be completing a corporate internship at Capitol Hill in Washington, DC, the powerhouse of politics. The chance to experience, up close, the political shenanigans in DC was a fabulous opportunity – or at least it would have been if the HR specialist responsible for organising the placement hadn't just been fired. Unfortunately for her, she had, so when Albert arrived no one knew he was coming. It was not his finest experience but, as bad as it was, it didn't come close to his WTF moment.

Albert had flown overnight from Heathrow, squished between two enormous sweaty sales reps, one of whom dribbled and snored like a train all the way. Then almost being mugged on the metro scared the pants off him. Actually, it may have been a misunderstanding with a homeless person, but it still shook him up. So he was a tad upset to be met with blank looks, no accommodation as promised, and no job to do – even if he'd had somewhere to sleep. So he did the smart thing and rang his mum. 'Just turn round, go back to the airport, use your return ticket and come back home' may not have been inspiring advice, but it was certainly practical. In the absence of a better idea, he made his way back to Dulles airport, taking care to avoid any homeless people, managed to book the next flight, and came right back to Heathrow. I'm sure that if he'd been away for months, either Mum or Dad would have broken a sweat to meet him, but he'd only been gone two days. So in place of a lift it was the Megabus home for Albert. He paid for his ticket and sat down on his case to wait for the hour to pass before his bus arrived.

Boom! This was his 'WTF just happened?' moment. A young woman walked past, trundling a huge case behind her tiny frame and sporting the floppiest hat he'd ever seen. It was a minor miracle that he caught her eye at all, but he did. Then something really strange happened. She trundled that case right behind him and walked round in a circle back in front of him again. He caught those twinkly eyes again, and then again. By the third time she circled him, he was wondering what was up. If that wasn't weird enough, she then spoke in a lilting West Coast American accent: 'Are you going to Rwanda?' Clearly she hadn't been practising her pickup lines. Albert, stunned for just a second, was able to stumble through a couple of sentences that basically communicated: 'No, I'm actually waiting for a bus to Birmingham.' A few minutes later he was embarrassed to discover that the real reason for the woman circling him and her rather odd question was that he was sitting directly beneath the 'meeting point' sign. He was right where she was supposed to be meeting the other members of the humanitarian mission who would be her travelling companions to Africa. Three hours later, after seeing her off through departures and having missed two buses home, he was sitting waiting for the next one, but this time feeling ever so much better than he had a few hours before.

Her name is Jenni. She too was nineteen and hailed from San Diego, but had been on a quickie tour of Europe along with her huge suitcase before leaving to do something to 'make a difference'. Jenni was also feeling ever so much better after meeting and talking to Albert for the last few hours. Instead of taking her last chance to binge on Starbucks before the Rwandan self-enforced coffee detox, she'd passed the time with a total stranger. The thing is, by the time she boarded her flight, he didn't feel like a stranger any more. For the next year they spoke two or three times a week on Skype, and when they weren't doing that emails were pinging across the Atlantic. It didn't feel strange then when, both having a desire to backpack through South America, they decided to go on a trip together. They 'connected' as planned, and what began as two friends discovering new parts of the world ended as two star-struck lovers, desperate never to part. The trouble was that, as neither had a job lined up or a company ready to sponsor them, in order to live together in either the UK or USA they would need to be married. They were young and in love, neither of them yet twenty-one. This time it was Jenni's mum who came through with real inspirational advice: 'You'll know if he's the one. You'll know you can be sure when there are physical fireworks like you can hardly believe, but – more than that – when those sparklers fizzle out, you aren't just friends, you are best friends. When you absolutely know that both are true, it won't matter if you're twenty-one or a hundred and twenty-one: if he's the one, he's the one. Think about that, and if it's right for you to marry, then you'll have my blessing.'

Jenni's dad, however, had a proviso. He insisted that they have coaching with the priest who'd agreed to marry them. Unusual, maybe, but as it turned out, very effective. After all, they'd both had to go home after the trip and were stuck with conducting an online relationship, thousands of miles apart – and everyone knows that out of sight often translates to out of mind.

They agreed, and for the next six months looked forward to the weekly Skype sessions with Father Thomas, during which he helped them to face the less glamorous aspects of married life: money worries, job stress, where to live, to have a dog first or a baby ... that kind of thing. As it happens, they enjoyed the coaching. So far, so good. They've been married for six years now, and appear more in love than ever. Chemistry and compatibility are essential, but a sensible approach to dealing with the reality of life is also a must. Put that all together, and it still doesn't guarantee anything, but it sure will help.

Evolutionary psychology confirms that there are basic neurological triggers necessary for one person to be sexually attracted to another. It also confirms that at a start of a relationship women produce more testosterone, making them more – how can I put this? – 'frisky'. During those rocket-firing, whizz-bang days, men have increased levels of the female hormone oestrogen, which makes them more caring than they might otherwise be. Eventually, however, these hormones change back. Therefore, it's almost inevitable that firework displays will tone down to maybe a spluttering lantern on a Sunday morning. Apparently.

Here's how to avoid saying yes when you should have held on for a while:

1   Ask better questions of, and about, each other. Some people take years to properly get to know each other, and by the time they do, they realise they don't like what they know. All you need to do is ask smarter questions: what do you want out of life? What would your perfect week/home/family/future/retirement etc. look, sound or feel like? What do you really want to avoid happening to you? What irritates you most in another person? What sexual fantasies do you have that you are scared to share? (OK, maybe not that last one, but you get the idea.) The more you know about another person and the more they really know about you, the more able you are to clear your mind and make a better judgement about your compatibility.

2   Recognise that liking is as important as loving. Love is a wonderful thing. I think most people agree with that, but ask them to define what love is, and you'll get a different answer from just about everyone you ask. Love is hard to pin down. Are there different types of love? Is loving someone and being 'in love' different? Does love blossom or is it just there? However, we all have a reasonably common reference when it comes to liking someone. We either do or we don't. They are either our friend or they are not. Things like trust, honesty, friendliness, compassion, reliability, intimacy — not in the sexual sense, but meaning the sharing of secrets, and just being able to 'rub along' together in companionable silence — are the building blocks of friendship, and long-term successful relationships need them.

3   Deal with tough stuff before it gets that way. It's no secret that life throws rocks in the road of blissful happiness, so why make talking about them taboo? You don't make bad stuff happen by talking about how you intend to deal with it; you make it happen by worrying about it and saying nothing until it's too late. Talk about it up-front and agree how you want to deal with it before it happens — not when it's already a problem.

How to avoid losing your way, and be successful despite the odds

WTF just happened to me? Wow, I'm a success!

Some WTF moments are fabulous – just ask John. On Monday he was a success, but a few weeks later, even with the world apparently going to hell in a hand-basket (in the 2007–08 global financial crisis), he was even more of a success! Whereas a financial meltdown was for some a WTF moment that caused their world to come crashing down, for John it became an unexpected opportunity. He's no hero in the regular sense, but he was heroic in his approach to dealing with something that caused most people to stop in their tracks and say 'WTF?!' Despite being faced with what looked like impending doom, John survived. He went from being a director of someone else's company and up to his ears in debt, to running his own show and making a success of his personal financial future. Good for John, eh?

Just about the only thing you can expect from the future is that the unexpected will happen, which is why so many people say that the way to make 'God' (if the idea of God doesn't work for you, then choose something that does) laugh is to tell Him your plans for the future. Funny, then, that so much money, time and effort is put into making five- and ten-year strategic plans. Governments and businesses all do it, and they make them sound so convincing that people believe them, even though they never turn out the way they were supposed to. Ordinary stiffs like you and me start making our own plans, which often rely on governments and big business, or at the very least are influenced by the things the government says will happen. Why do we do that?

John used to run a factory. Not a huge car-plant full of robots and assembly lines, but a more traditional, pre-Henry Ford type factory where real people built their bit and then handed it on for someone else to add their bit and so on until the final product appeared, all shiny, polished and ready for sale. Their production system may not have needed a moving conveyor belt, but that didn't mean the factory didn't have good systems, and certainly didn't mean the bosses didn't plan properly. No, sir, not this outfit. They operated with military precision and planned every step of their future. Unfortunately, their five-step plan didn't change very much:

1   Sell stock during the high demand period and continue to build.
2   Take all the money from the sales and reinvest most of it in new materials.
3   Build stock during the low demand period and hold it ready for demand to build.
4   Borrow money where necessary, and pay it back when the sales are made.
5   Repeat.

Everyone understood the plan and did their bit to make it happen. John's job was to make sure the stock was always being made, and plenty of it was ready for sale when demand was there. John was good at this, and did it well. Everyone on the shop floor knew what they had to do, and they too did it well. They all did it so well and for so long that they all had made their own five-step strategic plans. For some it was as straightforward as:

1   Go to work.
2   Get paid.
3   Pay bills.
4   Save for holidays and presents.

5 Repeat.

All was well in John's factory world. Until it wasn't.

Some personal plans, such as John's, were more complicated than a basic 'five-pointer'. John had three children, all in private schools, a mortgage that made his eyes water and a challenging relationship with his wife, as both had fiery tempers and arguments were a regular feature in the household. It's fair to say that home life could be a little stressful for John. He'd convinced himself that one day he wouldn't need such a huge house, and that one day he'd be able to afford to do more than 'rent' it from the bank with their monthly interest payments. This illusion had become a comfort blanket John could wrap around himself whenever common sense and logic nudged their way into his thinking. Therefore, he was not unlike most of the men and women on his shop floor. He tried not to think too far ahead – as long as the plan kept on working, everything was working. Isn't it amazing the way we convince ourselves that something has solid foundations when really it's all been built on the sands of our own fertile imaginations?

The day it stopped working was the day the house of cards came tumbling down. You see, what John, his fellow directors and the workforce didn't know was that the money they borrowed every year to bridge the gap between one season and the next didn't come from their friendly local bank manager. It came from a banking system that, if not technically corrupt, was less than fair. According to many media reports and 'post-crash' autopsies, some bankers knew (months before John's factory put itself in a vulnerable position) that it was all about to come crashing down around their ears.

The bankers didn't come out and take responsibility, they gave no advance warnings, nor did they make it easy for businesspeople like John to recover and survive. In John's case they had one response to requests for funding, and that was to say no.

Instead of stockpiling goods in readiness for the next season, as he would normally be doing, John laid off the whole workforce. Within weeks the directors took the decision to close for good a business that had been a going concern for generations. Within months the site it stood on had been vandalised and looted. The factory was gone. The taxes paid by the workers before they were forced onto benefits helped bail out the bankers, and within a year those same bankers were offering loans to firms like the one John had given his life to – and were back on their bonus schemes, of course.

Thanks to the banking system, John's plan had suffered a terminal hiccup, and John faced his WTF moment. No job, no business and, because there was no business, no pay-off or redundancy. The same bank that refused to keep his factory producing, now wanted to take his home away if he didn't pay his mortgage interest on the dot. The schools that appeared tolerant of just about anything the kids got up to had a zero-tolerance policy to non-payment of fees: no money, no school. It was as simple as that. As for his wife – well, she actually responded better than he'd imagined. All she demanded now was that he get another job sharpish. Easier said than done.

So, perhaps we might expect John to get divorced, be forced to live on state handouts, and to place his kids in schools that wouldn't have been his first choice. Well, that didn't happen. John's WTF moment brought home to him that relying on plans is *not* a good idea. He realised that he had not lost his way because some greedy money-hog in a high-rise somewhere in the corporate world had ripped off his future, but because he had failed to notice that the world he lived in was dynamic: failed to notice that it moves, it shakes, it shifts and it shimmies.

He'd always known it. After all, he had always been looking for a new, better way for the guys on the floor to do what they did, better and more efficiently. He had tried to never miss opportunities that took advantage of the latest technology. He knew things were constantly changing because change was what he did best. That's why it hit him like a slap in the face with a wet fish: WTF! John realised that he wasn't using what he knew. He'd lost his way because he'd forgotten that he was his own navigator, not anyone else. Not the bank, not the business, not the economy, only him. John knew that he had it in him to do something about it. He also knew what he had to achieve. He could see it as clearly as the nose on his face: he had to make his house secure, his kids secure and his wife … well, secure. Security was his goal, and he knew what that looked like. Some people would have whined, but not John. Instead he asked himself a better question: 'If I had no choice but to do what I've always believed could be done, what would I do?' He answered the question and soon knew what he had to do.

John is smart and has never been short of good ideas. He also knew a few people, and some of these people he'd been nice to over the years. They didn't exactly owe him, but he knew they would at least hear him out. John developed a new five-point plan. Not a strategic plan, a flexible plan.

Step 1. Find a backer.

Step 2. Get going.

Step 3. Keep going.

Step 4. Keep on keeping on going.

Step 5. If steps 1 to 4 aren't working, get a new plan.

John's plan worked, and it didn't take nearly as long as he thought it would. The result: John didn't lose the house, the kids finished school without incident, and his marriage was just fine.

It has been a while now since John's new flexi-plan kicked in. He is already on his third factory, and will soon be opening the first plant overseas. The people who caused the financial crash will never know that – indirectly – they did John a favour. John's factories create products that are making the world a better place. His employees, some of whom used to work for the old firm, love what they do, what they produce, and the difference their products make to the people who use them. While pretty much all WTF moments cause the heart to sink, it doesn't have to be so for long. John can attest to that.

Psychology supports what happened to John. Studies demonstrate that having a clear goal that you can clearly picture will make its achievement seem more doable because the goal will feel 'nearer'. If you are stressed, this leads to the production of adrenaline and a better focus on what you need to do, making positive action much more likely.

WTF Just Happened?

Here's how you can avoid losing your way:

1   Have you got your own flexible plan? Having a fixed plan is like trying to drive from London to Leith using only one route. When the road is blocked, you're in trouble. If this happens more than once, you may start wondering why you wanted to go to Leith in the first place. You may get so frustrated with such a rubbish plan that getting as far as Luton starts to look like a win, and you give up on the rest of the journey. If you set out with a goal and give up on the way, you have to ask yourself what you're missing.

2   Does your plan mean you're doing something that you like and that does you good? Does it lead to producing something that others will like and that will do them good too? Stamping your foot and demanding that the world treats you better is not going to work. Having a flexible plan means not just having enthusiasm, but enthusing other people too. You have to light their fire by engaging them in something they like.

3   Does your plan have wider implications that serve the greater good? Staying on course with your flexi-plan means that it has to be sustainable, and that means it has to do more than feed you and make a profit. That'll work for a while, but if what you produce doesn't have a lasting value, then you won't last either. Solar lights in a rainforest may sound like a great idea – unless you've actually been to a rainforest, that is. It rains. It has tree canopies that are higher than a block of flats, and it is dark most of the time, where you'd like it to be light. Whatever you do has to have a sustainable value for you to have a sustainable value too.

How to avoid crushing debt

WTF just happened to my wad?

Andy used to be an arrogant so-and-so. Now he is an unemployed, lonely, broke, arrogant so-and-so. Of course, I'm being polite because 'so-and-so' isn't the term other people have used to describe Andy. However, I'm not here to be rude to anyone, merely to point out things as they are, and to explain that anyone can have a WTF moment, whatever their personality. Fortunately for this so-and-so, he lives in a country that doesn't have debtors' prisons any more and affords basic human rights to all, no matter how flawed their character. Andy may have lost all his money, but he's also a pretty lucky so-and-so, even if he doesn't agree. It all depends how you look at it, I suppose.

A child I knew once remarked, 'My dad's mean. He won't buy me the new riding coat I need, and it's not fair because he doesn't have to pay; he can just put it on a credit card.' Out of the mouths of babes, eh? Yet this is exactly the subconscious programming that gets people like Andy into trouble. This isn't new, and it isn't unique to Andy; history is full of tales vilifying those who borrow more than they can afford to pay back, as well as those who are morally comfortable with lending more than they know can be repaid. I'm sure you don't need me to paint caricatures of the greedy spendthrift and the even greedier money-lender. Andy was the spendthrift.

Now, Andy may be a loser, but it would be unfair to single him out without making a much bigger point about the way we judge both borrowers and lenders. You see, if we talk about individual people you may have one point of view, but if we talk about whole groups of people – such as a country, for example – then we may have a different point of view altogether. So which point of view is the right one? For example, when Greece borrowed more than it could afford and kept on spending, with no hope of ever being able to pay back what it had already borrowed, it was inevitable there'd be trouble ahead. So while economists tell us that having some level of debt isn't necessarily a bad thing, having too much is gut-wrenchingly horrid. And those same economists tell us that it's actually necessary for modern economies to run on debt. Seemingly, it's the only way they can function, but are those 'rules' the same at a personal level?

Andy may have seen himself as grander than he actually is, but he isn't a country and therefore shouldn't have been playing by the financial rules that apply to one. Countries may never pay back their debt in any one person's lifetime. People, on the other hand, must pay back what they borrow ... before they die.

Loan sharks don't necessarily wear sharp suits, but instead issue plastic cards and advertise on daytime TV. Even so, they are still operating pretty much as they always did. They target otherwise smart people, who then fall into a pit of debt without necessarily realising they are doing it, and Andy was one of these people. He didn't start out with this end in mind and he didn't spiral into crushing debt on purpose. That's not to say it wasn't his own fault; it most certainly was. Andy was not just naive; he was stupid. For a clever bloke, he was dense. His ego was as big as the Tokyo Skytree, and he was totally out of control and self-absorbed.

To the casual observer, Andy was a successful young executive. He'd made partner by thirty and had married a stunning beauty by thirty-five. (As she was ten years his junior, this did wonders for both his ego and image among his equally shallow peer group. Not that marrying anyone younger is a problem in itself, but in this case Andy thought of her as another 'asset', and probably one he couldn't really afford.)

The attraction was definitely only skin-deep, and Andy knew it. He joked that marrying her was cheaper than having to pay for sex, which spoke volumes about the kind of bloke he was. Andy was not a nice person. He moved his bride into his penthouse apartment overlooking the Thames, and made sure they were seen at the best restaurants. He parked his Aston Martin as close as he could to the front door of wherever they were going, and if that happened to be a disabled spot then so be it; as far as Andy was concerned, if it was available, it was his for the taking. At work he treated his team like any of his possessions; they were there to be used and when their usefulness was fading, they were replaced.

It's probably no surprise that no one really liked Andy – not even his wife. They tolerated him either because they were afraid he'd fire them, or because the benefits of travelling in his wake were worth the crap that came along with it. However, all was not as it might appear. Yes, Andy was an egotist who deserved a slap for treating people the way he did, but he wasn't the success he wanted the world to believe. In reality, he was broke. He knew it, the bank knew it, his partners knew it, and yet he continued to live like everything he touched turned to gold. How did he do that? The answer is easier to understand when you look back at how getting into debt actually works. Andy had understood it, and had attempted to 'beat the system' by pinning other people's pain to his own. He walked a financial tightrope that – so long as he was careful – would keep him flying high.

He had maintained personal control of information regarding how much he owed, so that no one but him knew the extent of his 'exposure'. Loan companies offered him cards with massive credit limits, stores offered him their own credit cards and Andy, like so many people, got caught in a spiral of debt, borrowing so much that there was little chance of it ever being paid back.

No one had any idea just how much debt Andy was accruing, not even Andy. Before too long he was drinking himself into oblivion, taking whatever drugs he could get his hands on, and doing whatever he could to blot out the fear of knowing he couldn't keep the façade up forever. The tipping point for Andy came, as it does for many like him, when the balance of power shifted at work. As soon as it was easier to get rid of Andy than keep him, he was history. With his prestigious job gone, everything imploded almost instantly. In the space of a week his apartment had been repossessed, his wife left him, his car too was repossessed, and Andy was left with nothing. No possessions, no money, no friends, and no obvious route to ever paying off what he owed. All that was left for him to do was look around and ask himself, 'WTF just happened?'

> He blamed everyone but himself for the mess his life had become.

Unfortunately, Andy's story doesn't have a happy ending. It could have had one, but Andy remained angry and bitter. He remained a self-centred egotist who believed that rules are for other people and that the world 'owed' him. He blamed everyone but himself for the mess his life had become. Fortunately for Andy, he lived in a country that takes care of its own even when they don't deserve it. He had a roof over his head, food to eat and the opportunity to change, if he ever got past himself long enough to recognise it and do something about it.

Psychology tells us that debt is a form of overwhelm. Imagine a set of scales that have 'overwhelm' on one side and 'confidence' on the other; when more debt goes on the scales, it requires more confidence on the other side to keep the person in balance. The trouble is, of course, that thinking about dealing with the debt causes more overwhelm and less confidence, so the person becomes even more out of balance – and out-of-balance people do very silly things.

**Here's how
to avoid
crushing debt:**

1   Be clear about where you are right now. Having some debt is necessary ~ after all, very few people get to own their own home without having a mortgage. Clarity regarding your financial situation is essential if you want to stay in control. Most people fear their finances, and often for good reason. What they then tend to do is either see things as much worse than they really are, or much better than they really are. The answer is not to see things as better or worse than they are, but simply as they are. Embrace the truth. By doing this, you will ask better questions and will live with the reality of your finances. That will feel much better than the alternative.

2   Be clear about the difference between renting and buying assets and liabilities. Years ago my dad earned a bit of extra cash by working as a catalogue agent. That meant taking a printed catalogue of goods around his friends and family, from which they could buy goods and pay for them weekly, rather than all at once. They would buy cheap shoes that ~ with luck ~ would last six months, and pay for them over that same period. They paid the basic price, plus interest, and so were actually borrowing the money to buy the goods. Rarely were the goods reclaimed if the money wasn't paid, because the agent made sure the money came in, but technically they could have been. Today people rarely 'buy' their new (or even second-hand) car. They do a lease deal. They pay some money as a deposit and then pay an amount each month over a given period before having to hand the car back. They rent the car. The trouble is, most people don't sit in their new car and acknowledge they're in a rental; they talk about their new car as if it really is. It's not; it's rented. Buying a new house isn't acquiring an asset until you've paid for it. The bank owns it until your final payment; until then, those payments are a liability. Get real about what's yours and what's on the never-never.

WTF Just Happened?

3 Be clear about your intention each time you use a credit card. You will notice a huge difference in your buying habits if your intention is to pay off your credit card in full each month, as opposed to building up a debt. No one can make this choice about intent except you. Even if your credit cards are maxed out right now, it doesn't prevent you from intending to pay off what you spend. If you pay off more than the minimum each month, then at some point the debt will be no more. If your intent is to clear your credit cards, then every time you get a bonus or a little extra money you'll feel good about using it to pay off a bit more and eat into your debt. Hold the intention to get yourself sorted, and you will.

How to avoid losing your confidence and self-esteem

WTF just happened to my mojo?

Unfortunately, Ian's young wife and mother of their three children died. I suppose if anything is likely to burst a self-confidence bubble, it'll be something like that. Dealing with loss is tough, and the last thing I want to do here is make light of it. However, it does happen, and unfortunately we will all experience loss at some point. Nature tries to arrange it so that we lose our grandparents and then our parents, and even though we know it's coming and that it's an inevitability, many of us still try to pretend that it isn't. That loss can be devastating enough, but to lose your partner – someone you expected to be a permanent feature in your life – must be a squillion times worse. Ian's story is painful and raw, but it makes clear that 'mojo', confidence and self-esteem aren't reflections of what's going on in the world other people can see, but of your inner world, and are viewable only by you.

Stuff happens; everyone knows that. Most gets dealt with without a second thought. Or does it? I've never actually seen a straw break a camel's back, but I get the idea.

There is a tipping point for everything. You only have to watch kids at a party: two plates of jelly and ice cream? OK. One cupcake too many, and bleugh! One glass of wine over dinner may be OK, but a little more and the officer says 'Just blow into this, sir' and suddenly it's not so OK any more.

Ian has three children; Marie, Molly and Mary. Marie is twenty-three, Molly is twenty and Mary is just eighteen. Ian and Mandy were a fun couple and loved anything that brought a smile to their faces, even their own kids' names. When Mandy was diagnosed with terminal cancer, the whole family kept smiling through the chemo, through her final days, and even found a smile to celebrate her life at the funeral. Underneath their smiles, they were sad. They thought the sadness was passing with every smile, but it wasn't. The thing about sadness is that, on its own, it isn't enough to cause much more than vague feelings of moroseness that, with time, get covered up. When people say 'time heals', they're right, but just like any other wound it leaves a scar: sometimes one that can be seen, sometimes not. Losing a loved one isn't likely to cause a WTF moment, because it's all about dealing with the sharp pain of the moment, rather than reflection. So when Mandy died, Ian was so concerned with putting on a brave face for everyone else that he didn't have time for any self-reflection. When Ian's father died a few years later, the journey to his funeral was a sharp reminder for them all of Mandy's death. Ian's mum didn't last long without her husband of more than fifty years, so yet again Ian and his three daughters found themselves attending a funeral.

Being a responsible, mature human being and caring father, Ian carried his burden of sadness like a stoic. The girls knew Dad was sad, but didn't make a big deal of it. Mary had just started her first year away at uni, Molly was about to extend her time away with a master's, and Marie, who had already graduated as a teacher, had left home and lived in a shared house with a bunch of other young women. Life for the family wasn't over; it was just sort of flat: like a helium-filled balloon that bobs on a string and then sits in the corner of a bedroom and gets just a little less bouncy every day – not so quickly that you can see it happening, but each week it looks less and less cheerful. A balloon like that can hang around for months before it just gets so droopy and sad-looking that it has to be thrown out. Ian often thought of himself like that wilting balloon.

As he was a doctor, Ian knew the dangers of depression, and took his own medicine, both literally and figuratively. He wasn't being silly; the prescriptions were from a colleague, and he was careful. He also joined the gym and made sure he did something that broke a sweat at least twice a week. Even so, he was still that wilting balloon. The girls could see what was happening to their dad. Of course, nothing would ever replace their mum, and they too would always have the scars of her loss, but unlike Ian they had plenty of other things to stimulate them. The scar would always be there, but time was allowing it to fade. Ian, on the other hand, was unintentionally picking at that scar. The house hadn't changed at all since Mandy had died. The furniture was all laid out precisely the way she liked it. The carpets and curtains were the ones that she had chosen. The world had moved on everywhere but the place Ian called home.

Ian was still only in his fifties and was as physically healthy as anyone of his generation could hope to be. The mandatory trips to the gym kept him physically fit and although he never bought anything for the house, he did spend money on keeping up his appearance. He dressed well, had his hair cut regularly, shaved daily, showered every day, and never wore a shirt that wasn't perfectly laundered – something he'd had to master doing for himself. He was financially stable too. The house was paid for, his car was purchased outright, and if he'd wanted to he could have enjoyed extensive travel. However, seeing the world was something he and Mandy had always planned to do together, so he never really felt like going anywhere.

He may have dug himself into a rut, but it wasn't a rut with sides and a lid just yet. In reality, even though he was loath to think of himself that way, Ian was a bit of a catch. How many forty- or fifty-something single women must there be who'd find a good-looking, fit, healthy, financially stable, intelligent single man interesting? Ian wasn't a monk. He'd had sex since Mandy died, but it had only ever happened when he was away from home at a conference or meeting, and then only with women he didn't want to see again. So there was nothing stopping him having another relationship, except his own reticence and perhaps the continual picking of that scar. He was the camel loaded with straw. What had happened to him wasn't enough to break his back, but was more than enough to make the burden uncomfortable. Then it happened. The straw. WTF?! Crunch.

His eldest daughter, Marie, finally decided to take matters into her own hands. She loved her mum but hated going home because Dad wouldn't let Mandy go. He hadn't moved on with his life even a decade or so after her passing. The house looked like a museum dedicated to the memory of Mandy, and it shouldn't be. Mum wouldn't have wanted that, Marie knew. Indeed, she had been at pains to talk to them all about getting on with their lives after she was gone. Her death hadn't been a surprise; they'd all been at her bedside and been able to say goodbye. Marie and her sisters had taken their mum at her word and done what she'd asked: they'd got on with their lives, but Dad ... well, Dad was stuck. They'd talked and talked about doing something together: about going on holiday as a family, about all going away for Christmas, and about getting the house redecorated, but nothing ever changed. Even Mum's wardrobe was still full of her clothes, and that just couldn't be healthy. So Marie decided to do something about it.

Thursday was Dad's day for late consultations, so she knew he wouldn't be home till at least nine and would be out of the house as normal by eight in the morning. She arrived at her dad's house half an hour after he had left for work. Then her boyfriend Tony arrived. He would wield a paintbrush while she cleared cupboards and took bin bags of old clothes to the charity shop. Like a young Sarah Beeny (TV presenter of home makeover shows) on a mission, Marie pointed out the walls to be repainted – she had brought paint with her – and set Tony to work. She took a deep breath and started on her mum's wardrobe. Of course she cried, of course she had a lump in her throat as each dress reminded her of time with her mum, and of course there was a part of her that, like her dad, didn't want to let go; but she had resolved to do the right thing. Mum was gone but Dad was still here. She had no memories of any good times they'd shared since her mum had died, and Marie knew that wasn't the way it should be. She knew with all her heart that if her mum was looking down at her now, not only would she be cheering her on, but she'd be asking why she had taken so long to act.

By early evening, it was done. The makeover was just enough to brighten the place up. Some pictures had been replaced with artwork Marie had made herself, and others had been moved around. There were still pictures of Mum on the piano and above the fireplace, but there were new shots of the girls having fun too. The last thing they did was order a takeaway to be ready for when Dad got home. Marie taped a message to the front door saying she was at home and asking him to ring the doorbell rather than using his key – and then sat down nervously to wait. She'd sent Tony away earlier with the car as this was something she needed to do alone, so at nine-fifteen when the doorbell rang it would be just her and her dad. This was it – Ian's WTF moment happened as he opened the door.

At first it looked like things were going to go well. He was clearly pleased to see her, and they hugged. After that, things kind of went downhill. The first thing he noticed was the smell of fresh paint. Gently moving Marie to one side, he flipped on the light switch and stood stock-still, taking in the hallway that was his, but not his. Without saying a word, he opened the door to the living room and turned on all the lights. Still saying nothing and without taking off his coat, he moved from room to room, silently flicking on switches and leaving them on. Marie stayed where she was and didn't quite know how to react. This wasn't like Dad. He was normally so measured and logical. How come he hasn't asked a question or said anything? she wondered. Ian went up the stairs in silence. Marie heard the sliding doors to the wardrobe open, and then she heard something she'd never heard before. It was like a primal scream or a wolf's howl. Whatever it was it scared the pants off her, and was her turn to have a WTF moment.

They didn't eat the takeaway. Marie had sat in the kitchen on her own wondering what to do. Once or twice she'd ventured up the stairs, but could hear Dad sobbing in his room and had tiptoed back down again to the kitchen. She didn't know what to do or what to think or how to handle what she'd done. Had she been wrong? Eventually she'd settled down on the settee and fallen asleep.

She woke up to the sound and smell of breakfast. Dad was standing over the stove and the table was set for two, with freshly squeezed orange juice already on ice. That hadn't happened for years. Sensing her standing in the doorway, he pointed to the seat and simply asked, 'One egg or two?'

Weeks later, when all four of them had got together, with boyfriends for a family night out courtesy of Dad, he mentioned what a great job Marie and Tony had done with their choice of colours. That was it. It was the one and only time he referred to what they had done – but it didn't matter because Dad had changed. He even allowed the girls to help set up a dating profile for him online. Before long he was enjoying dates with some nice women, and not long after that Ian went from having fun with lots of people to having lots of fun with one person. He was never going to 'get over' Mandy – of course not. She was the love of his life, and that's something that would never go away, but that didn't mean life couldn't go on, and couldn't be fun. Walking through the door the night that Marie had painted his house, he'd had his WTF moment. All at once he'd realised that losing Mandy and then his own mum and dad had left him wounded and in pain – but not in enough pain to actually do something about it. Coming home to find that his daughter hadn't only noticed, but had taken time to plan and organise something to help, had moved him more than he'd imagined possible. Not only that, but he recognised that she'd also had to take a huge emotional gamble to try to help him, one that couldn't have been easy for her either.

He recognised that he'd been feeling sorry for himself, and this recognition had helped him get his mojo back: he'd made a decision to engage in a different set of behaviours, to focus on the future, and to simply get on with his life. He didn't 'snap out of it' or 'put it behind him', but he did decide to think about a positive future rather than a devastating past, use his facial muscles to smile instead of frown, and take every opportunity to be a better example to his children. He's making progress, and although not out of the woods yet he is at least heading that way.

Any psychologist will tell you that grief is tough to handle. The phases of denial, pleading, anger and acceptance will always be there, but the time it takes to go through each are different for different people. Some phases will pass quickly and some may cause a person to get stuck. Either way, your only hope - if you want to move on and allow the scar to form and then fade - is to get through them. Each phase can be painful; but just because people feel pain it doesn't necessarily mean they'll do something about it. There has to be more pain in not doing something than doing it before people are brave enough to do what's necessary.

Here's how to avoid losing your confidence and self-esteem:

1   Confidence is a feeling. Imagine there's a party going on. In one room people are politely talking about world events (boring); in another there are people dancing (fun); in another there are dark corners with sexy goings-on (great fun). Imagine you couldn't get to the party, but set up a video camera there instead. If it had been fixed in the first room you might not have been that bothered about missing it; if it was in the second room, it would stimulate a different feeling, and the third — well, different again. But here's the thing — it was all the same party. It's not what's happening that frames our confidence, but what we imagine is happening by how we frame it. Confidence is 'knowing that you know' no matter what the context or situation. Imagine that you are asked to talk to a stranger about something you are very familiar with. For example, perhaps you are good at making apple pies and are asked to explain how you make one. That shouldn't be a problem, should it? However, imagine that the person asking you is a top-class baker, a Mary Berry or a Paul Hollywood, and not only that but you are being filmed at the same time and broadcast to millions. Are you confident now? Maybe. If you are imagining yourself talking through your memory of making a great apple pie and are focused on the facts that you are confident you know, then it isn't

likely to be a problem, but if you start to imagine something different then there will be. If you imagine that the expert is already criticising you in their head, or that some of the millions watching are doubting your methods for apple pie making then might you start to doubt what you know? It is this doubt that causes a lack of confidence because your imagination is stronger and more powerful in controlling your thoughts than you might think.

2   Time doesn't make things better; you do. They say that watching a kettle makes it feel like the water takes ages to boil, but watching that kettle without turning on any heat will have you waiting forever, and it won't even get warm. If you want your mojo back, then you can't wait for life to light a fire under you; you have to light it yourself.

3   It's easy to lose your mojo. For as long as it is less painful to stay as you are, and more painful to look for your mojo, it will stay lost. The trick is to make staying as you are *more* painful than seeking your mojo.

How to avoid letting life pass you by

WTF just happened to my life of promise?

Alison compared herself to people she already believed were 'luckier' than she was. Is it any wonder, then, that she thought life was unfair? Her story will resonate with anyone who has made poor decisions when they were younger that they later came to regret, or at least question. The truth is that everyone starts off with a life full of promise. That promise may be easier to identify for a person born in the UK than for someone born into a country that's at war, in turmoil, or under the control of a despot. Even so, some promise will always exist. Alison was lucky even if she harboured a belief that she wasn't, and it was this limiting belief that caused her to let part of her life pass her by. Fortunately, Alison had a WTF moment in time to get back on track; and when you read her story I hope you agree that if she can do it, then surely anyone can. All anyone needs to do is figure out where they want to get to, and then allow themselves to believe that either they'll get there one day or die trying!

Imagine that every person is like a precious stone dropped into the pond of life. Their unique shape creates a unique set of ripples. Each and every thing that happens to them adds to the pattern of ripples. As life goes on, the pattern becomes ever more complicated and unique. This is why there are more than seven billion people on the planet and no two are exactly the same. Even identical twins only share the same genetic 'shape' when they hit life's pond, but never have precisely the same experience and ripple effect. Yet whatever corner of the world we live in, and however poor or advantaged our circumstances, some people make better use than others of the opportunities that come their way. Every experience presents a choice, but we have to be careful what we choose.

Fenella, Alison and Bianca were all in the first hockey team. Since becoming a formidable school force in Year Ten, the three girls knew that many other girls envied them, but were far too cool to acknowledge it was going on. Secretly, of course, they loved it. They certainly had lives full of promise laid out before them. Each was clever and didn't have to work too hard, but still got A grades. Each could hold their own in any conversation with teachers, parents and anyone of their own age brave enough to speak to them, and each was physically fit, attractive and full of the energy and enthusiasm of youth. But fast-forward five years, to the age of twenty, and things had changed. Fenella had done OK. Her acceptance at drama school led to a part in a UK-touring musical and then a lead role on an international tour of another musical. Bianca had also done well. She had missed getting a first by a whisker, and knew that the university hockey team post-match antics were probably to blame, but still landed a graduate job with a global conglomerate. Alison's life hadn't panned out quite so well, however. Already it was shaping up to be a mess. Fast-forward another five years and it was.

While her best mates from school had successful careers, and money, Alison had a different tally. Alison had an overweight seven-year-old with attention deficit hyperactivity disorder (ADHD), a failed relationship with his father, a marriage to someone she suspected was either bisexual and secretly seeing a man, a serial philanderer hitting on her girlfriends, or both, rent arrears for a slightly damp apartment, and a zero hours contract as a carer to old people. If there was a definition of an unwelcome outcome for a twenty-five-year-old, then this was it. Looking in the mirror didn't help Alison feel any better, because feeling good about yourself shows up unconsciously in the way a person looks and behaves. Once radiant, she was now sallow, blotchy and overweight, and her once cheerful smile had gone.

Fortunately for Alison, by surreptitiously listening to the local radio on carefully concealed headphones at work she had her moment of realisation. Because one fine day, as the song of that name was playing, she stopped in her tracks. Something about that song was reminding her of something that she couldn't quite put her finger on. What was it about 'One fine day' that was so familiar? Then in a flash of stunning recognition she realised what it was.

That's when Alison had her WTF moment. It wasn't the song that was familiar, but the singer. It was Fenella. The girl she had called one of her closest friends and believed with all her heart would be her friend forever, but whom she hadn't spoken to for years. The girl with whom she'd shared all her deepest secrets and fears would have no idea that while she was being interviewed from her Hong Kong hotel suite about the musical she was starring in, her once best friend felt stuck doing a job that may suit some people, but wasn't what she'd once imagined as her career. That's when – *Bang!* It hit Alison like a bolt of lightning. She just stood there, listening to her friend, hanging on her every word.

All Alison could hear herself saying was 'How did this happen? How could I have ended up here doing this, while Fen is out there doing all that?' These were not necessarily the best questions she could have asked, but were at least a start. Hopefully they would be the precursors for questions like 'What can I do about it?' and 'What must I start doing differently so I can start living a life that's closer to the promise I know I have?' Only Alison knows what she asked herself, but what was apparent was that she began making changes.

The first thing she did was reconnect with Fenella and Bianca. She made a point of not complaining about her own life, so as not to appear jealous of theirs. She neither made her life sound better than it was, nor worse; she just told it as it was. This worked, and both girls warmed to her immediately without any need to make comparisons about how well they'd done. For the three most image-conscious girls in school, the lack of any comparisons now was nothing short of amazing.

The effect it had on Alison was also amazing. She ditched her errant husband and saw a divorce solicitor. She ditched her rented flat and moved back in with her parents. All the bitterness and frustration she'd aimed in their direction previously was gone, and any resentment they might have felt melted away as she openly and honestly admitted to the mistakes she'd made. She ditched the job in the old folks' home. In fact, Alison ditched everything about her life that wasn't going to help her achieve the promise she now knew she had.

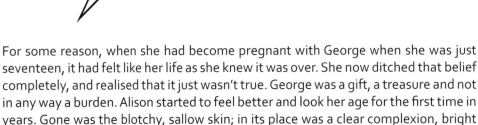

Alison ditched everything about her life that wasn't going to help her achieve the promise she now knew she had.

For some reason, when she had become pregnant with George when she was just seventeen, it had felt like her life as she knew it was over. She now ditched that belief completely, and realised that it just wasn't true. George was a gift, a treasure and not in any way a burden. Alison started to feel better and look her age for the first time in years. Gone was the blotchy, sallow skin; in its place was a clear complexion, bright eyes and pearly white smile. Gone was the lank and greasy hair, as her soft auburn curls got their bounce back, and gone was the frosty, belligerent attitude she now realised she'd adopted, which acted like a barbed-wire fence around her. Alison's self-esteem shot up like mercury in a baker's oven, and 'hot' was exactly how young men started to see her. Enrolling for a degree with the Open University was her first step on the road to promise, and being offered a part-time job as a personal assistant came next. Making her parents proud had happened as soon as she'd ditched her old life and come back home, and her parents supported her with every step she was taking now. It was as if someone had turned on a switch and suddenly everything had changed. Life really would never be the same again.

For years, psychologists have recognised that subconscious beliefs are the equivalent of a human satnav. Whatever a person believes is true, the human brain will do its best to accommodate. For example a person desirous of buying a new piece of furniture will unconsciously be looking for opportunities to buy it; they will notice stores that sell furniture, be drawn to adverts in magazines or newspapers that are promoting furniture sales, or will unconsciously tune in to TV adverts for furniture even if in the midst of a conversation. It may feel as if the universe is answering your need to buy a new sofa. That might be a fun idea, but in reality it is your unconscious pattern-matching system bringing things to your attention. Imagine you didn't want a new sofa and ask yourself if you are as likely to notice the stores, be drawn to the adverts, or be interrupted by the TV? Just like when you enter a destination into a satnav, your beliefs act as your destination and you can't help but be drawn towards them.

As long as a person allows themselves to believe that their life is a certain way, then it will stay that way. Yet as soon as that person changes their belief to one that allows them to do something different and better, then miraculously life starts to be different, and more often than not it gets better.

WTF Just Happened?

Here's how to avoid letting life pass you by:

1 Recognise that what you do is actively shaping the person you are. Human beings develop patterns of behaviour that they can't help repeating. Honestly, we can't help it: if you've ever been to a free seating conference and then left the auditorium for a break, which chair do you go back to? If the conference is for more than one day, which chair do you head for the next day? The same one, right? We are all creatures of habit, and we like patterns, so think about whether your patterns and habits are helping or hindering you. Is what you are doing right now taking you closer to, or further away from, what you really want?

2 Recognise that yesterday can't be changed ~ but today can. Why do so many people become fixated on what's happened rather than using their time to figure out what they want to happen next? Guilt about mistakes, shame about bad decisions, and the fear of being found out are just some of the reasons why people spend more time looking back than forward.

3 Recognise that if one person like you can do something amazing, then so can you. Not everyone is lucky enough to be born into a society where everyone goes to school, and where having your own mobile phone is considered a necessity by the time you're ten. The problems with reaching your full potential are going to be different in the Borneo rainforest than they are in a Birmingham suburb. So comparing the two is irrelevant. Comparing the lives of people from similar backgrounds and similar circumstances can't tell you everything you need to know about your potential, but can offer up useful clues. Luck is simply the meeting of opportunity with preparation. So be prepared.

How to avoid misinterpretations, mistakes and misunderstandings

WTF just happened to the instructions I thought I'd given?

Derek thought he was Teflon Man: invincible and untouchable. He wasn't. However, while this story is about Derek and his apparent hero syndrome, it's actually more about the guy who hired him. You see, it's like this: the person who hired Derek, a guy named Jeremy, did so because he needed someone else to do his dirty work. By stepping over the line of appropriateness, he had relieved himself of the power to either restrain the antics of an ego-crazed female manager or fire her. Therefore, he'd sought out a 'trouble shooter' with a reputation for taking tough action. He imagined such a person would have no problem digging him out of the unprofessional hole he'd dug for himself. However, Derek's image of himself wasn't going to allow that to happen. His vision of himself was that of the 'ultimate professional', a person hired to handle difficult management situations that needed his specific brand of expertise.

Derek expected the person who hired him to provide a clear brief and then allow him to do his job. He had not expected to be hired as a means for a senior manager to cover up inappropriate behaviour between himself and a more junior employee. Derek had hoped that this would be another notch on his professional bed-post; another successful outcome achieved by Teflon Man, who steps into the stink of organisational chaos and comes out smelling of roses – but it wasn't to be. Jeremy had hoped that hiring Derek would see an end to his self-made inappropriately intimate problem and that Derek would step in and 'deal' with Jessica, but poor old Jeremy was wrong.

He was wrong because he pretended to himself that one thing would lead to another, giving him the result he wanted. He saw the world as if it were a stack of dominoes standing on their ends, just waiting for one to be pushed over. The trouble is, we don't live in a linear world where one thing just follows another without interference, but in a dynamic world where unseen and unimagined things come from nowhere. Derek's fit of conscience came out of left field and was Jeremy's undoing. He probably figured it out, but way too late, that assumptions within instructions are not a good idea. What he should have done was be clear, because the three most important aspects of being understood are (1) the clarity of what's requested, (2) the clarity of what's interpreted and (3) the clarity of what's understood.

Clarity is the missing link between what you think you said and what someone else hears. 'When you have time, will you take care of that, please?' can mean 'Why haven't you done that already?', 'Don't make me tell you to do that again', 'Why didn't you recognise that needed doing without me telling you?', 'Get it done now', or maybe, although I doubt it, 'Wait until you genuinely have nothing else to do, and then if you feel like it, do this please.' Sometimes, for the sake of decency and good manners, we cloud our instructions on purpose: 'Don't point, darling, it's rude' may be a better way of preventing embarrassing comments from your five-year-old than waiting for them to point out that the lady on the bus has a beard.

This is a story about three people: Derek the hard-nosed pro, Jessica the hard-faced pro, and her boss, who wasn't a pro at all. Derek is a management 'gun for hire': his expertise was in facilitating the removal of a person from the payroll, legally and honourably, but also permanently. For a while, this was a blast. Derek really enjoyed his work. He believed that people were the creators of their own destiny, so if he had to sack someone, he believed they deserved it. He didn't question whether what he was doing was right or morally justified. He'd been hired to do a job and he was good at it. End of. Unfortunately for Derek, it wasn't 'end of'. The older he got, and the mores scalps he collected, the more uneasy he became.

Derek had overheard someone talking about him and using the term 'hero syndrome'. Not knowing what that was, he Googled it and at first was irritated that anyone could think he actually created problems in order to fix them. However, the more he reflected on those scalps, the more he couldn't help but wonder if he'd been just a little too enthusiastic about finding reasons to end careers. As he mellowed, he wondered if a more compassionate, more relaxed, and more genuinely self-assured version of himself might solve more problems, and maybe even save some careers.

There had been many times when Derek was faced with one person's word against another's about who was responsible for whatever failure had led to him being brought in. The only way Derek knew how to deal with this was to be straightforward; if a person knew about a problem before it happened then he held them responsible regardless of rank or responsibility. If they didn't know until after the event then he gave them the benefit of the doubt, even when the responsibility was clearly their own. He thought he had tried to be a fair and honest broker on behalf of whatever company had hired him. However, fairness was not always quite so simple or straightforward.

The more Derek sacked people, the more he couldn't help thinking how he might feel if he was in their position. His nagging feeling that finding a way to be right and proving to be 'fair' were two very different things came back again and again. Of course they were all numpties, but maybe they didn't all deserve to have their lives torn apart on the whim of a new boss, or to feed someone else's ego. Derek had begun to doubt the integrity of his own approach, which was not a good thing for someone who does what he did for a living; if anyone had to be certain about themselves, to be clear about what they said and did, and to be arrogant enough to believe in their own infallibility, it was someone like Derek.

Now is a good time to introduce Jessica. Jessica was a mean piece of work: there's no two ways about it. Some people might have explained away her behaviour as being the result of poor self-esteem. If the rumours were true, and in several cases they were, that might be the cause for her attempting to sleep her way to the top. It was a strategy that appeared effective for a while, anyway. It hit a road-block when one man wasn't taken in by Jessica's obvious physical charms, and refused to 'play by her rules'. Unfortunately for the company and everyone actually deserving of promotion, he moved on when his part of the business was 'merged' with a competitor.

Of course, Jessica was convinced that his reticence to become involved with her must be because he wasn't attracted to women. The fact that he had a lovely wife, three children and a happy life didn't feature on Jessica's landscape. Her world revolved around her, and only her. I told you – she's self-obsessed, manipulative and arrogant: behaviours probably driven by a horrible lack of personal self-worth and a fear that letting down her guard might allow others to see how weak she really was. Not that this was any comfort for those on the receiving end of her nastiness. If that sounds harsh, you may be assured that I am actually sugar-coating reality for you. She was way worse than I'm making out! On top of that, she wasn't that bright, and believed that people could be manipulated without them being aware of it. She was like one of those people who go to a live concert, sit in the front row and talk about the performer in loud whispers as if those on stage can't hear. They can. Comedians have the opportunity to yell back: 'It's not the bloody telly, you know; I can see you!'

Yet however difficult and challenging Jessica might be, Derek had been hired by her boss, apparently to help her reduce the head count. Derek, who at this stage had no inkling of Jeremy's Machiavellian plot, couldn't help but assume that Jeremy must know about Jessica's shortcomings. He was curious why she didn't feature in his brief. It was very odd, because Jeremy must have known that Derek would see immediately that it was Jessica who ought to be first out of the door. It didn't take Derek long to figure out that something else must be going on.

The something else was that, as much as Jeremy still enjoyed the odd night away 'on business' with Jessica, he was aware of her personality, and had hired Derek to do what he now felt unable to do. Either make Jessica see the error of her ways and change, or change her for a new employee so that no one else had to experience the error of her ways any more. Jeremy was conflicted because he genuinely did want to do the right thing. On the one hand he wanted to do his job properly and look after the interests of the company, on the other he had become accustomed to the cosy arrangement between himself and Jessica and was loath to change it. What it boiled down to, and the reason Derek had been hired, was self-protection for Jeremy: he didn't trust Jessica to manage the team and he knew that if he attempted to intervene she would turn on him quicker than a rattle snake and bite him just as hard.

Jeremy needed someone like Derek to make sure that appointing Jessica didn't end up being the cause of his own downfall. Derek was expensive, but worth it if he kept Jessica from costing Jeremy his career. Clearly, Jeremy didn't trust Jessica. He was well aware that she was sneaky and might try to use Derek as her personal corporate hit-man, targeting the careers of those she didn't like and supporting only those who did as they were told and averted their eyes in her presence. He knew Jessica was a bully but hoped that Derek was smart enough to handle her. Jeremy might have hoped that Derek would be his insurance policy, and Jessica was determined to use him for her own ends. While it might have looked like Derek was between a rock and a hard place, it didn't take him long to figure out what was really going on.

Now, don't go feeling sorry for Derek. This wasn't his first rodeo, so to speak, because he had handled tough situations before. He'd been around long enough to realise what Jeremy was really scared of. He was super scared that a whistle-blower would take the opportunity to try to not only take down Jessica, but him too. When all was said and done, Derek was smart; he wasn't way out of the ballpark with his take on the situation, but he did misjudge how dreadful Jessica really was. If Derek hadn't misjudged the extent of her self-destructive treachery, then things might have turned out differently. If Derek had been more open and less judgemental about Jeremy and less judgemental about himself and his own fears about his hero syndrome, then maybe he wouldn't have done what he did. You see, Derek had his WTF moment when all his pent-up frustration at being Mr Fix-It for undeserving bullies like Jessica welled up until he could hold back no more.

Derek lost it because he'd had a bellyful of Jessicas and Jeremys, and needed to do something. He may not have chosen this route again, but it's always easier to make a better call with 20-20 hindsight. Every person he spoke to had the same story: 'The operation would be far more productive and this conversation wouldn't be necessary if Jessica just got out of the way and let everyone do what needed to be done.' Staff were 'all so fearful of Jessica and her moods that politics was more important than productivity' and that 'being seen to be doing something by Jessica was far more important than actually achieving anything – as long as Jessica was off your back you could stop worrying'. All Derek heard was Jessica this and Jessica that. Yet here he was, reviewing each person's performance before deciding whose high flying career was about to be shot down in flames. It hit him like a bolt through the brain. This was not the time to blindly follow a superficial brief. This was time to decide what his instructions really meant. He needed to think about what he'd actually been instructed to do, and then figure out how to do it better than he was now. Which is how Jeremy also ended up having his own WTF moment.

Derek, having reviewed his own instructions, made up his mind; he decided that productivity improvements were at the heart of the brief, and that while they had been issued by an individual they were actually issued on behalf of the organisation, which he took to mean that it was within his brief to interpret them in the best way he saw fit. In effect, he rewrote the instructions to match what he felt he needed to do. He declared to himself that this time there would be no hero syndrome, no making things worse just so that Teflon Man could appear to make things better, because this time he was determined to do the 'right' thing.

With this as his aim, he then produced a detailed report that made recommendations about what should change, who should go, who should stay, and what needed to be done to improve productivity. In it he made it abundantly clear that it was in the organisation's best interest to free up the future of Jessica and Jeremy, and allow them to further their careers outside of the company. This he then hand-delivered to the group's chief operating officer. A meeting followed, then another and another. At the time all Derek could say was 'Jerry Maguire, eat your heart out!' because, just like the film character who risked all by putting on paper what he genuinely believed as opposed to what he imagined his bosses wanted to hear, he too was risking his own career by drawing attention to a bad situation that had been allowed to deteriorate further because of poor management. In hindsight, that may have been a mistake.

Jessica and Jeremy were never seen again at the company. Their desks had been cleared and a short memo had been issued wishing them well in their future careers, wherever that might be. Derek hadn't been involved in their exit from the organisation but, to his surprise, he was retained by the company, at least for a short while.

They recognised that Derek was an asset; his clarity of thought and the questions he'd asked in relation to the brief were considered exceptional. He didn't stick around long at that company because as much as they heaped praise on him at the time, afterwards everyone with a secret to hide was wary of him. So he moved on and picked up other Mr Fix-It gigs, but he was never quite the same again. There was no more 'hero syndrome' for Derek. He was, in fact, better; he was an improved version of himself. He always searched for clarity and understanding, tried to do whatever was necessary, but do it for the 'right' reasons, and he relished the fact that he'd had a WTF moment that had changed him for the better.

Psychologists will tell you that clarity of thought almost always determines action. All words have two meanings: the semantic 'what it would say in the dictionary' meaning, and the episodic 'what happened to you the last time you heard that word'. This means that nothing you say can be taken at face value because people use different dictionaries and hardly ever have the same experiences. Add to this the fact that brains take in all manner of information that the person is not aware of, but which affects how they behave. Hypnotists call it an 'unconscious embedded command' when an instruction is taken in without the person realising it. Machiavellian managers call it manoeuvring, but whatever label it's given it all boils down to this: we hear, see and feel everything that we come into contact with. However, even though we consciously remember only the tiniest portion of it, all those bits we don't remember still affect the way we behave. Therefore, the only way to cut through all the unconscious stuff is to be clear about what you are saying, what you mean, and what you want.

WTF Just Happened?

Here's how to avoid being misunderstood:

1 Know what you want and why you want it. The more clearly you articulate what you want and the outcome it needs to produce, the better; but that's still not enough. To check meanings, you have to ask what the other person thinks you mean, what they think you are asking for, and what they think the outcome you want looks, sounds and feels like. If you don't ask the right questions, then you should expect to get something different, something you weren't hoping for.

2 Be prepared to take action yourself as well as demand action from others. Being misunderstood is as much about energy and enthusiasm as it is about what you are asking to be done. It's common knowledge that 'it ain't what you say, it's the way you say it' that matters – and nothing speaks louder or with more resonance than actually taking action yourself. You can tell your children to keep the house tidy, but notice how much faster they take notice if you are seen tidying wherever you go. Leading by example isn't a pithy phrase; it's a means of getting your instructions carried out without misunderstanding.

3 Be flexible when things aren't working out. If you hear yourself saying: 'I've told him/her already, and it still isn't done', then stop doing what you're doing, because it isn't working. Instead of getting uptight – or, worse, giving the same instruction again but this time louder – start being flexible. Do something different. If this approach doesn't work, try something different again, over and over again until it does. Of course, that doesn't necessarily mean persevering with the same person. One of your flexible approaches may be to fire somebody. The point is that the only way your instructions can be misunderstood is if you let them be. So don't.

How to avoid getting taken for a ride

WTF just happened to my common sense, my focus and my reputation?

Oliver didn't have that much to start with, but panicking meant he ended up with nothing: no money, no reputation, nothing. Did he have it coming? You decide, but before you hear his story allow me to point out what happens to anyone who gets taken for a ride: confidence tricksters no longer stand on the back of a horse-drawn wagon selling dubious medicines, nor are they confined to email scams trying to convince you that you've inherited a vast fortune and to send them details of your bank account and passwords. There have been – and probably always will be – different cons, from counterfeit branding to cold-callers masquerading as bank clerks wanting your account details, but they all have one thing in common – they prey upon the common human desire to get something we don't have and that we want. It doesn't matter if it's money, fame, or even hair regrowth that you desire; you can be sure that somewhere out there on the internet there's a confidence trickster hoping to 'get you'. Oliver's story isn't one of greed or avarice, just a loss of focus: if you take your focus away from what you really,

```
truly want, in favour of something that looks easier or
faster or cheaper, you will fail.
```

Once upon a time, people lived in a land of anonymity where the only way a person could become well known was to get their face in the paper or be on TV. Then, in less time than you'd expect, the world changed. First, there was the internet for geeks. This was a clever way of connecting computers so that they could communicate with each other by sending data back and forth through phone lines. Then came the internet for less geeky geeks. This allowed people to set up web pages that could be looked at from any computer just by signing into the internet. Suddenly, we were not anonymous.

Oliver wasn't born in the UK. In his native country, he'd been successful in business and had been hired by a large corporation. Steadily working his way through the management ranks, he first headed up a regional office, then reached the heady heights of their national head office before being given an overseas posting and reaching the peak of his corporate career as a divisional director in the north of England – not bad for a lad who'd started with no formal education in business. Along the way he'd acquired everything he needed on the education front: he'd completed a degree in marketing and then a master's in business administration, both funded by his company. Oliver had it made: a flash company car, a generous expense account, a loving family and a luxurious home. What could possibly go wrong?

Redundancy was what went wrong. The 2007–2008 global recession bit deep into the corporate world. Many people were made redundant – and he was one of them. At first it didn't look so bad. As he'd been with his company for years, he'd earned a healthy golden parachute and it looked like he'd have plenty of time to find a new job. Unfortunately, new jobs for an expat in his kind of role were hard to come by. Oliver was by no means the only person to have been chopped, and they were all fighting for whatever opportunities came along. Most of these new jobs paid way less than they'd earned previously but, the tougher it got, the more willing Oliver's competitors were to take whatever was offered.

Oliver wasn't. Oliver thought he had a better plan. Oliver was wrong. The more desperate he became, the more he lowered his standards and the worse the damage to his reputation was, and a damaged reputation can take years to recover, if indeed it ever does.

As it became clear to him that he wasn't going to walk into another cushy job, he began to panic, and in that state of panic he came up with his new plan. It was not a focused plan, or a well-thought-out plan, just a 'new' plan. Now, you probably don't need me to tell you that coming up with a new plan when you're panicking is not likely to end well. Coming up with any plan isn't smart when your pulse is racing and adrenaline is shooting through your veins. Coming up with a career plan that involves spending all that remains of your severance package is even less smart, but that's precisely what Oliver did. He was attracted to a promise of 'easy money'. It seemed too good to be true – and of course, it was. This new plan of Oliver's meant him spending every last penny on a brilliant 'business system'. A means of making money that apparently had been tried and tested all over the world and was helping companies make millions. It wasn't a get rich quick scheme or one of those pyramid sales cons, but a cleverly constructed approach to running any business, made up of training manuals, business planning tools, and even sample letters to prospective customers. To a business novice it looked like a treasure trove of money-making goodies, but to a more experienced person it was nothing more than could be cobbled together with the assiduous application of Mr Google. Oliver wasn't a novice in business, but he was a novice to 'small business'. His whole life had been spent as a small cog in a series of much larger wheels. All he had ever needed to do was be good at his specialism, but when faced with starting a business on his own he needed to be good at pretty much everything, at least to start with.

Perhaps if he had stopped to ask if the same system had been applied to the company he was buying from and if it had worked for them, he might have realised that this was more likely to make his bald patch grow new hair than earn him the fortune he was looking for because the franchisors were not rolling in financial clover. Had he been around the small business block a few more times he probably would have realised that they needed his money more than he needed their product. It's not as if Oliver had only himself to worry about. He had a wife and two children, who were very small at the time, to consider. He lived in a rented house and was quite literally the equivalent of two pay cheques away from being out on the street. Yet, rather than secure his situation and live to fight another day, Oliver was consumed with the desire to get back on top. He was more concerned about being seen as successful by his cronies than almost anything else. This need to be seen as successful, combined with his panic about apparently having few choices, was a potent mix and led to a complete loss of focus. Clearly, if he had been focused on where he wanted to go, rather than panicking about the mess he was in, then he probably wouldn't have done that. However, hindsight doesn't help when the money has been spent.

Here's the thing: the ideas the franchise company were selling him were actually OK, and if they could be implemented in an organisation they probably would have improved performance. There was, however, a big *but*: those ideas weren't new, nor were they confined to that franchise. Was it true that the franchise seller had done lots of work in providing various templates and questionnaires that the new franchisee could use? Yes, of course they had, but were those forms and archived information of any more practical use than buying a few good books from a management bookstore or consulting Mr Google? No, not really. Add to that the fact that there were thousands of out-of-work executives just like Oliver, all willing and able to share their expertise as consultants with whoever would pay them, and the result was inevitable: no one except gullible new start-ups would buy what he had to sell, and as enthusiastic as they might have been about Oliver, they couldn't afford to pay him more than a pittance.

Before too long it became obvious even to Oliver that he had been sold something that did what it claimed to do – but only if he could sell it. The franchisor claimed an honourable deal had been struck, and that if Oliver could not sell their wares then that was due to his poor salesmanship and not their poor product. It was an argument that would go nowhere. They already knew there was no way poor old Oliver was going to challenge them in court, because he couldn't afford it. He was well and truly up a gum tree without a paddle.

Oliver's website proclaimed him to be an expert advisor with expert tools and expert credentials. It meant that the expectations of potential clients were high. He knew he couldn't meet those expectations with the rubbish he'd invested in, but what choice did he have? He had nowhere to go and no choice but to try to make the best of a bad job. The more he tried to sell something he knew was not that great, the more people got that same feeling too. It's not something you can hide. People are equipped with a sophisticated computer-like brain that finds you out: neuropsychology links emotionally important issues with an unconscious pattern-matching system, in Oliver's case: 'is this person selling me something that's worthwhile?'

The brain picks up all manner of clues that we are consciously unaware of, and it puts them together so they make sense. This is similar to the way the brain processes shapes and turns them into faces, or 'edges' and makes them magically appear as tables, chairs and buildings. It matches tiny clues about your expectations of a person and checks if they pan out. The expectations of Oliver's clients didn't match up with what they were seeing. Unfortunately for Oliver, once a set of 'warning clues' have been identified, then we start to see them ... everywhere. All these unconscious clues were telling people that Oliver's self-advertised reputation wasn't deserved. No one should be surprised that his business bombed: Oliver still limped on, and scratched out a living. It was a shame, because Oliver was better than that, and each day he looked at his life and asked, 'WTF just happened?'

What happened is that, instead of focusing on the job he wanted, he allowed himself to be manipulated. He can't get back what he has lost; his reputation has changed because of the things he's done, but he still has the opportunity to shift his focus from where he is to where he wants to be.

Psychologists have demonstrated that the clearer a person imagines an outcome, the nearer it will seem to be. It doesn't matter if that image is good or bad, merely that it is clear. Therefore, a person with a brand or image that is lacking in clarity will find it difficult to attract people, because they will feel too far away, and too difficult to engage with. It therefore pays to be very clear about who you are, what you do, and what you can do for other people – but beware: think of it like travelling to a destination you've been to many times before. The first time you make the trip it may feel like it takes ages and that your destination is a long way away, but once you've familiarised yourself with the journey and made it a few times, the time it takes to get there can feel shorter (even if it's actually not) and the destination can feel nearer. That's why it is important to be clear about your image – it is your destination. If it is unclear it'll always feel a long way away, but once you've established clarity then you are already on your way.

Here's how to avoid letting your reputation go down the pan:

1   Be your own spin doctor. Even if your product isn't the best in the world, it doesn't stop you from being the best you you can be. A private contractor, advisor or consultant is successful because he meets, and continues to meet, the expectations of the people doing the hiring. They care more about you meeting – or exceeding – their expectations than they do about anything else, which means establishing (conscious and unconscious) expectations must be your first priority. If you are not a world-famous guru on your subject, make sure your web page doesn't make you out to be. If you are an expert in just one aspect of business, don't claim via your literature and online presence that you are an expert on all aspects of business, because if you do, you'll be caught out, even if your clients aren't trying to catch you out.

2   Be on the top of your game: you owe it to yourself to be the best you can be. The first person you let down won't be your client; it will be you, if you allow yourself to lag behind your own potential. Everyone has different potential so don't go assuming that anything is possible, but you can assume that you are unlikely to have reached your full potential just yet. Think about your own potential and ask yourself just how good could you be if nothing was preventing you from being at your best? Once you've figured that out you should recognise that whatever you are achieving right now is probably falling short of what you could be. If so, there must be something getting in the way of you reaching that potential. You can't reach your potential if you don't look for those barriers, but you also can't be on the top of your game if you pretend someone else's game is linked to achieving your potential. It's not. You are in control of being at your best, no matter what mistakes you've made or what crazy investments you might have made. You own your potential.

3   Be on message all the time; to be 'on message' you need to know what the message should be. You need to know what you are trying to say and what you want other people to see and hear. Once you have clarified what that message is, it's up to you to look at all the material you put out, all the conversations you have, and all the promises you make. You decide what needs to happen to be 'on message', so it's up to you to keep your communication in alignment with your message.

How to avoid getting dumped all the time

WTF just happened to my dream of a perfect relationship?

Being a hopeless romantic isn't something to be proud of – just ask Steve. Steve, bless him, was (and probably still is) a hopeless romantic: 'To live for today and love for tomorrow is the wisdom of a fool, because tomorrow is promised to no one' is how Sir Tom begins one of his classic tunes. No doubt it was a big hit because of his amazing voice, but perhaps the words hit a chord too. OK, they might be a tad cheesy for a songwriter today, but back in the 1960s and 1970s people were up for plenty of 'cheese'. These were the transitional years from flower power to the next generation, which was led to believe it could achieve anything and have anything it wanted. Therein lies the kernel of the problem that caused the divorce rate to skyrocket and made one-night stands culturally acceptable. People from those generations are parents and grandparents today, and millions of them suffered the ignominy of being dumped, not just as teenagers, but after years of seemingly happy marriage. These are the people who struggle with the concept of both living and loving in the moment, as opposed

to constantly imagining that there might be something better around the corner. While I'm in the song lyric mood, I'm
not suggesting that 'if you can't be with the one you love,
love the one you're with', because this too suggests that
your real love is somewhere else, and implies that someday
you might get the 'one you really love' as long as you keep
on looking.

Somehow the concept of finding a partner and loving that person through thick and thin morphed from being a joyful and fulfilling experience to being stoical. The 'baby boomer' generation (and beyond) wanted more than stoicism from life; they wanted it all. The trouble is that this translated into a life of 'searching'. Don't misunderstand me – I'm not suggesting everyone felt that way, but this need for something better, this constant looking over the shoulder to see if the grass might be greener, is at least to some extent to blame for family break-ups.

Steve was typical of that generation. Neither male-model material nor plain, Steve was pleasant-looking, with a quick wit and the propensity to become the life and soul of the party after a couple of drinks, at which point he would fall in love with the first girl who smiled in his direction. He fell in love too quickly, without really knowing the woman he was with, which scared women off. Psychologists might argue that his desire to find a life partner while still in his teens was the result of his own parents' break-up, but it could have been caused by anything. He was only sixteen when he pledged his love to a twenty-year-old shop assistant and ran away with her in her ancient Ford, with only a tent to live in. It lasted a couple of weeks until she had emptied his savings account and got fed up with sleeping on a groundsheet. Angry and disillusioned at being dumped, and after making himself look a complete fool in front of his family, Steve put on a brave face and made up his mind that he wouldn't let that happen again, but it did. With his mindset, particularly after a beer or two, it was inevitably going to happen again ... and again ... and again. He did manage a year or so of one-night stands and drunken liaisons on front-room sofas, but it wasn't long before his heart had been stolen again, this time by someone he was sure he could never have. It was as if Steve's unconscious had told him that, to survive, he needed to live for today and love for tomorrow, and that the pain of unrequited love was better than being in a fulfilling relationship, because it saved him from even more pain further down the line.

Then Steve met Dianne and sparks flew in all directions. They declared their love for each other and after dating for a reasonable amount of time got engaged. Steve was still the life and soul of the party and still a 'good guy', but he was also still suffering from 'what next?' syndrome. He didn't embrace his current job without focusing on what would come next; he wasn't interested in making the most of where he lived because he was already thinking about what would happen when they moved; and although he loved Dianne he always had an eye for the ladies – and, whether he knew it or not, was giving signals that he was up for an affair. So, while Dianne undoubtedly loved Steve, she also listened to her instincts. She needed stability and did not spend time worrying about 'what next?' as so many of her generation did, including Steve. The perfect storm of Steve working away from home, Dianne's instinctive doubts about him, and being approached and flattered by a much older man (who appeared the epitome of stability) meant that she ended up dumping Steve. Although hurt, Steve took it in his stride, as if it was what he had expected.

Steve went on to get involved in another relationship immediately. He never married, but had a string of relationships and four children to whom he is an absent father. His role as life and soul of the party has now been replaced by a reputation for being a drunk with a dangerous temper. He has few friends, but many acquaintances. He lives with a woman he doesn't love – and he wouldn't admit it openly, but he is deeply unhappy. He is still living today and loving for tomorrow. He is still a victim of his own view of the world, one in which he controls a relationship by being prepared for it to end, expecting it to end, and almost wanting it to end.

The sad fact is that Steve probably belonged with Dianne. If he had loved for today as well as lived for it, then he would have fought for Dianne and could well have won her back. Of that I'm reasonably confident, because her own marriage hasn't lasted, and she too became a lost soul in search of something she'd once had, but lost. She too appears to be living a life that includes being serially dumped: never happy with whatever she's got, she complains until her new partner has had enough. She sees it coming, but carries on being difficult even as disaster looms, and, although she might not admit it, I'm pretty sure she starts every new relationship assuming that she's going to get dumped. For Steve and Dianne, it's a self-fulfilling prophecy.

Steve and Dianne are two people among millions who have suffered the same fate. They had unconsciously asked themselves terrible questions, questions that caused them to believe their only course of action was a bad one. Dianne probably asked herself: 'What if I commit myself to him and he leaves me?', and Steve probably asked: 'What if she decides to leave me? Aren't I better prepared for that if I'm expecting it and already on the lookout for what's next?' These were damaging, life-altering questions for Steve and Dianne. However, if either of them had asked: 'What can I do to love this person even more today, put my trust in them even more today, and forge ahead with a future with them even more today?' then, I believe, they would have had a much better chance of still being together today. Getting serially dumped doesn't happen by accident; you have to try really hard, by repeating the same mistakes that got you dumped before. You have to suppress any romantic notions that you may have had, just in case they hurt you again, and you have to ignore any chance to change and just expect the world around you to change instead. Here's a newsflash – it won't.

Psychology tells us that the notion 'I think therefore I am' has its roots in brain science rather than philosophy. We all create our own mental versions of reality, and it happens first in the mind and not 'out there' with other people. Never is that more true than with long-term relationships: the relationship must first be successful in the minds of those who are part of it before it can be in real life, and this happens as a result of the habitual questions each of those people ask themselves. Every human being navigates through life by asking themselves questions. The questions we ask are more powerful than most people realise, and deserve not to be left to chance.

WTF Just Happened?

Here's how to avoid being 'let go' by someone you want to hold on to:

1   When you find a person you truly love, then love them completely. If you can't give your love, it's not because they are doing something wrong, it's because you are either trying to love someone who is not right for you, or you're being controlled by some other unconscious drive that's distracting you. Figure out which it is, and deal with it. If you are not with the right person, then do both of you a big favour and part. However, if you are holding back for any reason then deal with it: get help, talk it through, meditate or do whatever it is you need to do to fix it, because if you don't it will hurt you.

2   Think of each day with this person you love as being a gift. Imagine what it would be like if they weren't with you, and do everything you can to make sure you play your part in getting on with loving as well as living in the moment. When you treasure every moment, even the ones where you argue or disagree, as something that is meant to be part of your life together, then you will see them for what they really are: a real, genuine gift and something to be treasured. The more love you give, the more you will get, and if for some tragic reason the person you love is taken away from you, then at least when they're gone you will have no regrets.

3   Treat your lover as well as you would your best friend, and consider them a partner, not an acquisition. Life partners are not a thing you own; they are their own person. People don't think of their best friends as anything but a person in his or her own right, to be treated with respect. If you want your love to last, then you must treat your lover with at least the same respect you do your best friend. Forget that, and you will suffer the consequences; you will eventually be dumped.

How to avoid losing out at work

WTF just happened to 'my' promotion?

Rupal was really miffed when she didn't get 'her' promotion. You see, it wasn't *a* promotion, it was *her* promotion, and so it must have felt like someone had taken her toys away. Therefore, Rupal's response was to throw the rest of her toys out of the pram – metaphorically speaking, of course. Her WTF moment happened when she realised the promotion she expected was going to the youngster she'd trained. She was more than just a mite peeved, and wasn't going to take it lying down; she was going to sort it. At least, that's what she imagined would happen. However, rampaging around like a wounded lioness in the workplace isn't likely to achieve anything more than scaring the life out of everyone. Blame and frustration may be comfortable bedfellows, but they don't achieve very much, and certainly didn't help Rupal get what she wanted.

She didn't get the promotion that she, her peers, and almost all her subordinates (except, of course, the one who leapfrogged her and actually got the promotion) thought she had in the bag. How did that happen? It must have felt like just weeks since she had been given the wide-eyed enthusiastic trainee to mentor and train. Clearly, time flies when you're caught up with just getting on with the job; the next step up the ladder she thought was hers for the taking has been snatched away, and the person doing the snatching is using the skills Rupal spent years figuring out, but which didn't take nearly as long to pass on. Rupal had a choice: to face the truth that she wasn't the best fit for the job, to sink into depression, to rage against the injustice, to withdraw into passive-aggression, to put it down to experience and soldier on, to be grateful she at least had a job, to suppress any negative feelings, allowing them only to surface at home, or to do something else entirely …

However, Rupal had a blind spot. She was self-obsessed. Whatever came up in conversation, she always seemed to turn it around to what *she* thought, and what she would do if it were her. She would twist any conversation so that she could talk about herself and her plan. I know that her friends would start a random conversation about something obscure and place bets on when Rupal would turn it into something about herself. They were never disappointed. Rupal seemed to think that her ideas were always right and that whatever happened she would have a plan for it. She was mistaken.

She hadn't figured out what to do yet. She hadn't come to terms with the fact that Rachel would soon be taking over the US office, and it would be Rachel, not her, who'd no longer be suffering the commute to work by Tube. Rupal imagined that Rachel would soon be cruising to work in some flash open-top motor, and with every image she created she got angrier and more frustrated. Inside her head she was screaming 'WTF?!' For at least the past year she had set her sights on living in Los Angeles, and thought she'd done everything necessary to land the job. She hadn't made a secret of it, either: everyone from the night cleaner to the CEO knew that she wanted the job. The fact that it wasn't hers was a blow. That it was to be run by that young woman, supposedly her junior, felt like a slap in the face.

Slaps and blows are not an over-exaggeration when describing how it feels to be passed over in favour of a junior colleague. There's no doubt that it can be irritating to miss out on a plum job to an outsider, particularly if it looks like they're no better equipped to do the job than you are. Of course, there's always the chance that they have some additional distinction of which you're unaware, but that thought isn't uppermost when someone gets 'your' job, and you've been the one training them and teaching them all that you know. When that happens, it isn't an exaggeration to say that it feels like a punch in the gut. Rupal did feel well and truly punched. She felt the punch, the slap and the blow, and responded by throwing a tantrum. It wasn't pretty. Apparently she started reasonably calmly, and then lost the plot. Unfortunately for Rupal, this merely served to prove to Jane, Rupal's boss, that making the decision to put Rachel in charge had been the right one: the US office needed a safe pair of hands, a manager who behaved professionally and who could cope with disappointments, not a firecracker apt to burst into flames whenever she didn't get her own way.

Rupal did not respond well. 'It wasn't fair, and I wasn't going to put up with it! Jane has never liked me, and I'm sure this was her way of getting back at me for proving that I'm smarter than her. I'm going over her head. I'm going to let them know that they have an incompetent manager here who is suppressing talent. I'm going to knock Jane off her pedestal, and then kick her when she's down. She doesn't know it, but I recorded some of the client meetings we had, so I can prove that, when we got a result, it was actually me who made it happen, not her. Then I'm going to blow the whistle on that brown-nosing Rachel. She doesn't deserve a promotion any more than Jane deserves to keep her job; they're both going to suffer after I've finished with them.'

True to her word, Rupal made a formal complaint about Jane's handling of the appointment, then went on to make another formal complaint about other aspects of Jane's behaviour, including that she had falsely taken credit for business achievements that should rightly have been attributed to Rupal, her evidence for which was the recordings of several client meetings. In addition, she submitted a summary of performance as an addendum to Rachel's performance appraisal. None of her complaints or attempts to malign her junior went down well with anyone. At best, they were considered a lapse of judgement, and at worst, as immature and petulant. However, because the complaints were made formally they had to be officially investigated. After extensive interviews and much paperwork, Jane was cleared of any wrong-doing: unlike Rupal, who was found to have made unfounded accusations, recorded confidential client meetings without authorisation or the permission of the client, and had shown a lack of respect for the organisation. Rupal may one day think herself lucky that they didn't fire her; instead they agreed leaving terms, gave her a reasonable severance package, and magnanimously wished her well for the future.

If they think she learned her lesson, they are wrong. She is still fuming, still blames Jane, and still thinks she was right to do what she did. Unfortunately, that probably means she will do it again. Poor Rupal – when will she learn?

A good psychologist or business coach will tell you that it's never an 'issue' that causes a problem; it's the 'structure' surrounding it. In other words, the context and circumstances are one thing, but the approach you take to deal with them is another entirely. It is perfectly possible to have two people go through a similar set of events; the first reacts badly and responds with their gut reaction as each event unfolds, the second has more structure to their thinking, perhaps by ensuring they are clear about their desired outcome and adjust their responses as events unfold in an attempt to get as close to it as possible. The first person responds to issues, the second tailors their responses to a structure. If you want to put out a fire, you have to remove the sources that feed it, not argue over who started it. When it comes to being promoted, there are many structures to consider, but first are the needs of the person doing the promoting, and the organisation. These needs ought to be the same, but may not be. The smart candidate for promotion serves the needs of the person doing the promoting and then, and only then, ensures they align with the needs of the organisation. A pragmatic approach ensures the job gets done, whereas a pedantic approach doesn't get you promoted, and without promotion you won't get an opportunity to take care of the organisation's goals. Let go of issues, focus on your outcome, and then serve the structures that will put that outcome within your grasp.

Here's how to avoid getting passed over in favour of someone less 'worthy':

1 Be at your best by recognising your strengths and working on them. We all have strengths, but often take them for granted. People can get so caught up in worrying about what they *haven't* got that they forget all the good things that are already theirs. Strengths often go underutilised or unnoticed for years, which is a waste, so identify your strengths, figure out if there's any way you can utilise them even more, then start using them. It doesn't matter if you're not sure how to use them more: just start trying anyway, and you'll learn as you go along.

2 Be true to yourself and address any critical weaknesses. We all have weaknesses, and it's a mistake to focus on them at the expense of your strengths. However, if any of those weaknesses are going to stop you from being successful, then you had better recognise them, and quickly. Not only must you know what they are, but you must then do something about them. Make a plan and get on with it. If you are not sure what the plan should be, then just pick an approach and go with it. If it's not the right one, you'll find out soon enough, and then you can switch to the correct one.

3 Don't be a pain in the arse when you don't get your own way, even if you truly believe you have been wronged. Instead, get over it, and get over it quickly. If someone has wronged you, then trying to wrong them in return won't help. Not only do two wrongs not make a right; they cause people to get fired, and can really mess up their careers. Remember, you're never going to be at your best when you are disappointed and frustrated, so give yourself space, and take some time to reflect on how to make the most of your situation. If you do go into battle you're not going to win, and when the dust settles the biggest loser will be you, so don't do it.

Here's the thing: weight is a big – huge – and growing problem. It's not unkind to point out that saying one thing and doing another isn't helpful if you want to stay in shape, nor is behaving inconsistently limited to the overweight. Lisa and Duncan spend so much time talking about diet and exercise that they don't have any time left to actually do any. Without meaning to, they have become 'professional losers'– and not the weight-loss kind. If you hear the cry 'WTF?! Who ate all the pies?' well, it might not have been Lisa and Duncan, but it sure looks like they did, and they could have avoided this if only they'd been more aware of what they were doing at the time.

Lisa and Duncan are both overweight. Lisa is lucky to have no medical or psychological factors that might prevent her having a body shape that's fit and healthy, nor does Duncan. Even so he seems to spend his life in the doctor's waiting room, even though there's nothing wrong with him apart from the self-inflicted results of over-indulgence. He gets sick more often than a fit and healthy person does. His doctor suggests that losing weight will help relieve the pressure on his knees and that a more balanced diet might help his immune system deal more effectively with whatever bug happens to be doing the rounds. Of course, Duncan insists that his regular visits to the surgery have nothing to do with the excess pounds he carries, no matter what medical advice he receives. Unfortunately, not only is Lisa not in shape, she's not healthy either. You could say that Lisa and Duncan were made for each other.

If a couple like Lisa and Duncan are happy, in love, good together and don't do anyone any harm, then good luck to them. However, if they whine and complain because they don't want to be fat, unfit and unhealthy, then they are likely to attract criticism (even if it is said in hushed tones behind their backs for fear of offending or being labelled 'fattist') simply because they are hypocritical; they say one thing and do another. In this, they are by no means alone.

Lisa and Duncan, and all the other couples who are just like them, I know you don't like hearing it, but you know it, I know it, and everyone you meet knows it, and no one wants to hurt your feelings because you are a very nice person, but the reality is: *you are overweight*. Sorry, and all that. I know it's a taboo subject, and it's not my intention to be rude, but let's get real here: the Lisas and Duncans of this world need to either build a bridge and get over it, or do something about it. Remember, unless there really is a medical reason for being overweight it is either a positive choice 'I'm happy this way, leave me alone', in which case, of course, no criticism intended, it's your body, your life and your choice. Or it's because they choose to be because they've given up on finding a means of changing their behaviour. I'm not suggesting for one moment that changing behaviour is easy, far from it. However, there is absolutely no doubt that it is possible once a person has found their personal 'motive for action', their motivation. Anyone who claims changing their behaviour is not possible is more likely to be saying 'I don't know how to find my motivation to do it', and unless I'm alone in my experience, there are lots of people like that. It's frustrating for them, I get that, but for goodness' sake, if they project their frustration onto other people just because they point out the truth about their weight, then they're likely to stay fat, but if they focus on what they want, and find their motivation, then perhaps, one day they may find themselves in better shape.

If you relate to Lisa and Duncan, then you too will have had that moment when you looked in a mirror and said 'WTF ... I'm fat!' You could dress it up, I suppose, and use language that hides the truth, but if you are fat then you're fat, so step up, grow up and man up (that goes for women too!) and say it as it is: you are ... fat. OK, use 'overweight' if you prefer – I'm not intending to be rude, just clear.

If you've slowly been putting on weight, for whatever reason, then one day you may catch a glimpse of yourself and realise the truth. There's no getting around it; you can see it and you can feel it. Nothing in your wardrobe fits, and however much you breathe in and from whatever angle you look at yourself in the mirror, you are what you are. Your wobbly bits are out of control!

How the hell did that happen? You religiously drank diet drinks, only had the occasional 'treat', and surely didn't eat anywhere near as much as it must take to get this big, so what happened? It's not fair, that's for sure. Yet there it is: fat, clinging to you like baby poop to a picnic blanket. Now, let's figure out what to do to fix it – and better still, how to then avoid a similar WTF moment happening again, simply by being brutally honest with ourselves and raising our own awareness of what our own actions do to us.

Before we do, it might help to hear how easy it is for this to happen, and how even those in the diet and weight-control business can end up in the same boat. Yes, I'm talking about Lisa. You see, Lisa is a bit of a legend. She runs a weight-loss self-help group, and has done for years. It's where she met Duncan – and even now he still attends every week as both a group member and as an unpaid helper. Her group love her, which is probably why they come back week after week, even though their weight goes up and down like an out-of-control rollercoaster. She has her own way of running a group: her group doesn't attract serious dieters, but is a magnet for others who love the company of people just like themselves – overweight people who would rather be in the company of other overweight people than do something constructive about it, like spending a few hours in the gym, going for a brisk walk – anything that helps use up energy instead of simply listening to someone talk about some theory or other about how they *might* lose weight. Sitting and listening doesn't shed the pounds, but actually moving a bit may do. Lisa's view is that it's better to be in the group and trying to shed extra pounds than giving up and leaving. If a member happens to have had a bad week, Lisa is apt to say something like 'There's no shame in a gain' or 'There's always next week.' Lisa is very forgiving, as long as fees are paid every week.

Lisa clearly values effort, or at least purported effort, above actual success. Whereas one might expect the leader of a slimming group to be setting an example and demonstrating what is possible, Lisa just gets fatter and fatter. She can't be more than 5 foot 2 inches, and has to weigh in at 14 stones. Laughing off her lack of self-achievement in the field of weight loss, she describes herself as being 'in shape' – because, after all, round is a shape too. Duncan just sits quietly wrapped in the comfort of his overlapping chins and listens to Lisa preach the gospel of weight loss. She preaches a scripture of diet and exercise from her weekly pulpit, proffering advice about how to stay 'on track', as if she were already her ideal weight and could run up a flight of stairs without looking like she's about to explode.

Lisa ignores the fact that going on holiday has pretty much become a thing of the past, because the man she lives with has to squeeze himself into his seat on an aeroplane and then still overflows onto the seat next door. It's not nice, and it's not because the airlines are making the seats smaller, nor are 'people in general getting bigger'. I feel bad for them, but me feeling bad and then not being honest won't help them – nor anyone else in their position. They are all going to have a WTF moment and it won't be pleasant, so surely it's better to try to do something positive rather than just wait for the inevitable?

If you are also saying one thing, doing another and then you're unhappy because your clothes appear to be getting smaller, it's burying your head in the sand and ignoring the issue that's caused you to end up like you are. Lisa and Duncan found a way to *pretend* that they were making progress towards their goal of being in great shape by comparing themselves to other people who are also unsuccessful. Unsuccessful equals loser, and making a loser your benchmark is bound to make you a loser too. If the person you compare yourself to is someone who eats more than you do, works out less than you do, and blames everything but themself even more than you do, then you are comparing yourself to a loser.

Losers who have caused you to avoid winning. The truth is that if you want to avoid being a loser and actually want to lose weight instead then you have to compare yourself to a winner. You must figure out what 'a winner' looks like, sounds like, and acts like. Your winner might not be a skinny supermodel, so don't compare what you do to what she does. But someone who looks great as far as you are concerned, who wears their clothes with style, and clearly gives the impression of being happy and healthy – this is your winner. This person may be bigger than the winner someone else chooses as their winner, but that's OK – this is your life we're talking about, not theirs. Winners know what they are doing and are happy with it, whereas losers simply don't, and it's not about any particular choice: there are as many ways to change your shape as there are stars in the night sky. Slimming clubs have their regimes, and there are countless diet books and celebrity plans, but none will have any effect until you decide to change your identity and start comparing your every move to the version of yourself you want to be – that version of yourself you consider a winner.

People make decisions using a thinking hierarchy. Purpose is at the top and identity just below it, underneath that are beliefs, values, abilities, knowledge, behaviours and everything that makes up the environment. This was proposed and developed by Robert Dilts and then Gregory Bateson.* It works like this; imagine two people start arguing at work. Fred is a good guy and has been doing a good job for some years, he is respected and liked but since Ginger arrived he has been moody and sullen. While never openly rude to her he has been passively aggressive, which led to her becoming frustrated and more than a little irritated with him. It reached a head when they argued openly in the office with raised voices, upsetting their co-workers and leaving them unsure how to deal with either Fred or Ginger. It appears that a possible cause for Fred's bad temper is that Ginger, who is new to the company, was allocated a better and bigger office than his, with natural daylight that his doesn't have, and so from the moment they met, Fred was frosty and Ginger responded by being wary of him. The boss began by starting near the bottom of this pyramid by trying to fix the environment; 'What if we get Fred a bigger office?' was never going to be a successful strategy. Nor was getting both of them in and 'banging their heads together' and telling them to act like grown-ups. Nor was sending Fred on some kind of training course and giving Ginger some coaching in assertiveness. The problem was probably way up the pyramid and had something to do with the situation conflicting with their

* See http://www.nlpu.com/Articles/LevelsSummary.htm.

values or beliefs – Fred's about how he was perceived by the company, and Ginger's about her co-worker's respect, or to do with their individual identities – with both Fred and Ginger seeing themselves as 'the kind of person who doesn't stand for this kind of behaviour', albeit in different ways. If the boss wanted to be sure of getting either of them to change they must be asked questions near the top of the pyramid; questions like, 'Is this behaviour representing who you really are?' Ultimately, at the very top of the pyramid sits the thinking level of 'purpose', so ask 'Is the inevitable outcome of this behaviour the result you really want?'

Purpose sits at the very top of the thinking pyramid and that's why a person committed to achieving a weight target for a specific purpose can be so determined and so focused on achieving it, whatever the cost or changes they have to make. However, not everyone is as driven or has such a strong, purposeful approach to losing weight. Just below 'purpose' in the hierarchy is the level of 'identity', which is something everyone has, and identities can be easily influenced by people we compare ourselves to. Compare yourself to losers and guess what, you stand a good chance of developing the identity of a loser. Lisa, bless her, is a loser, and so is Duncan. Her group and her husband may enjoy the weekly weigh-in and community of commiserators, but they're lessening their chances of winning at the weight-loss game as long as they stay there. Sorry, Lisa – as lovely as you are, you really aren't helping these people be as successful as they could be, because you aren't helping them be honest with themselves, and you're not helping raise their awareness of their own actions. It's not good enough to talk about what they should do when you don't set a good example by doing it, and, second, they don't need to focus on what they should be doing, but on the purpose they really want to achieve. This is not a weight-loss goal or a number of points scored in a week or some such drivel, but a meaningful and purposeful outcome – if they fail to achieve it, it will cause them serious emotional pain.

Emotional pain is not like physical pain. It is the hurt a person feels for letting themselves down, the shame they feel for failing to live up to their own standards, or the embarrassment of saying one thing and then doing another. When a person links an action to an emotional pain then that action will change. For example, when I was growing up I sang in a choir. Not just any old choir mind you, a full-blown Cathedral

WTF Just Happened?

Boys' Choir that was so serious about the quality of the choral music we had practice sessions four mornings a week before school, before singing evensong on Saturday, and then before singing during Holy Communion on Sunday morning and evensong on late Sunday afternoon. A big chunk of every school holiday from the age of seven to almost fifteen was taken up by being the visiting choir in other UK cathedrals and overseas. As a young boy I sang solo perched high in organ lofts, or at one end of a cathedral trying desperately to keep time with a choir so far away that there were tiny delays in hearing them (you have to concentrate very hard on the conductor's baton and do your best to only listen to yourself).

I look back now and ask myself, how did that happen? What caused an ordinary boy to commit in such an extraordinary way? The answer was not in any 'carrot or stick' style promise of reward or punishment, but in the clever way the boys of that choir were shaped into peer groups; each year's intake formed bonds with each other, and when performing together the whole choir became one big team, all focused on achieving a single goal. If a boy was late for practice he wasn't punished but was quietly asked if he felt his behaviour was fair to the others who relied on him. When preparing for a recording session or a concert we would all be required to sit quietly, relax and picture ourselves performing at our best. There was no pressure on us, but I realise now that we were set up to put appropriate pressure on ourselves; not to push beyond our boundaries, or to be under stress, but to simply be the best we could be. To *not* do that was to feel the emotional pain of letting ourselves and our friends down. No one has to join a choir or a team to feel the benefits of emotional pain. All you need to learn to do is find a better way of asking yourself powerful questions, and a great tool to help you to prioritise those questions is the thinking pyramid.

To recap, there is a pyramid of thinking levels developed by Robert Dilts and Gregory Bateson and often referred to as the 'neurological levels of thinking'. It sounds rather grand and technical but in reality it is a simple way of thinking about how people prioritise their thoughts. It suggests that when a person thinks at any one of the levels in the pyramid, it is a more powerful thought than anything that might take place in the levels below. Focusing on plans, understanding how many calories are in this or that, and what level of fat or sugar is in something doesn't necessarily lead to success. What will lead to success is when your identity is consistent with what you want to achieve. Get clear about the identity you want for yourself and have a clear purpose so that you have attached an emotionally relevant meaning to achieving that identity, and you won't be turning around and asking 'WTF just happened?' when you look in a mirror.

Try these better questions, to avoid getting fat:

1   What physical shape do you *really* want to be in? Not the shape you would kinda like to have if it wasn't too much trouble, but the shape that you absolutely *have* to have for you to live happily.

2   Who do you know, or know of, who is already the physical shape you want to be, and appears to be able to maintain it without apparent effort? In other words, don't choose somebody who has to have regular coffee enemas or needs to climb mountains to stay fit. Choose somebody relatively 'normal' to aspire to.

3   Find someone who is an example of how you would like to be, and then ask yourself if it's possible for you to do whatever it is they do. Of course, this means you have to have a way of knowing what they do, so choosing somebody you see on the way to work, or who you've admired from afar in Starbucks, is going to be a challenge. 'Excuse me, I read this great book that had me ask myself way better questions, and one of them means I've got to know how you manage to stay in such good shape' is probably one of the worst chat-up lines in history and may get you arrested, so be smart about who you choose as your 'exemplar'.

How to avoid losing when you should have won

WTF just happened to my success?

Leroy let his ego ruin his life. He missed tons of opportunities, but he still can't see it.

Remember what it was like to be fifteen, and now imagine sitting in a lecture theatre being told how to be successful by a forty-something bloke sporting greying dreads and multi-coloured trainers, and wearing a Beyoncé-style head mike, even though there are only fifty of you in the room. What might you be thinking? Might you be sitting there saying, 'What the heck was he thinking?' Hmm ... methinks you wouldn't be alone if you were.

Leroy is the guy on stage, and his story is a salutary tale. No one is a machine, not me or you and certainly not Leroy. Unlike machines, people make decisions based on emotions, not logic, and Leroy is no human laptop. He'd like to think he's always taken a sensible, grown-up approach to those important decisions he's made, but the truth is that he only got all clever and intellectual about them *after* he'd pretty much decided what he wanted to do anyway. Unfortunately, what Leroy said he wanted, and the decisions he made, never matched up. He'd have been better off relying on his laptop.

It's a crying shame, because Leroy was a bright kid with a wealth of opportunity. He could have really made something of himself but it was clear to everyone but Leroy that this wasn't going to happen without a decent education. If he'd been a laptop he would have worked hard at school, got into university and probably entered the world of high-earning grown-ups pretty quickly. However the dull reality of college, university, internship and then a career was not for Leroy. Oh no – he had a different agenda made possible by an accommodating father. Leroy's dad had got used to getting his own way without question, and he had very definite ideas about what his kids needed. He didn't believe in giving his kids a head start by giving them money for the best education; perhaps he wanted to prove that his own rise to fame and fortune hadn't been a fluke by pushing his kids through the same meat-grinder and hoping that they came out like he had, so what Leroy's dad did was to make opportunities available for his offspring to learn good 'life lessons' by going to the same seminars and courses he'd once attended himself. He didn't force them, but if they were so inclined to go on trips to exotic destinations like Hawaii and Fiji, funded by the 'bank of Dad' then they could. Is it any wonder that Leroy gave real education a body-swerve and did this instead? With nothing more than his dad's credit card and a suitcase, Leroy started out on a world tour of life learning.

Now, you may be thinking, how was Leroy any different to any other backpacking kid, apart from his unlimited credit card? Well, the difference was that Leroy wasn't intent on diving the Great Barrier Reef, dancing naked at a full-moon party, or gawping at the Grand Canyon. Leroy was genuinely following in his father's footsteps on a journey of personal development and spiritual discovery. He did actually attend seminars and workshops by self-help gurus across the globe, just like his dear old dad had. Leroy wanted to float on underground lakes, balance on the highest bendy poles, walk barefoot over glowing coals, and absorb the wisdom of the ages – and he wanted to do it all before he was nineteen. He may not have been as smart as a laptop, but there was no doubting Leroy's passion. Not only was he passionate, he was also determined.

He was committed, no doubt about that too. He was also massively in denial. If anyone dared ask him which university he was going to attend after his wisdom-acquiring trip, he would bite their head off and snap that university was for 'other' people, and that he didn't conform to the rules laid down by other people, and other such opinionated clap-trap. Although amusing at first, it got boring after a while, and it was clear to everyone except the young and feisty Leroy that something else was going on with him. Something very emotional, that was causing him to respond like a child who'd been told to go to bed, before play time, without his favourite teddy. Most of his fellow seminar-goers had earned the right to be there; they had already made their squillions or saved every penny to be with their guru. That Leroy hadn't done this made him appear even more like a spoiled brat, and yet of them all it was Leroy who was the most arrogant, boastful, opinionated and forthright on his views about life and the best way to live it.

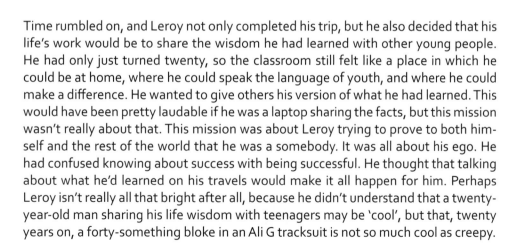

He had confused knowing about success with being successful. He thought that talking about what he'd learned on his travels would make it all happen for him.

Time rumbled on, and Leroy not only completed his trip, but he also decided that his life's work would be to share the wisdom he had learned with other young people. He had only just turned twenty, so the classroom still felt like a place in which he could be at home, where he could speak the language of youth, and where he could make a difference. He wanted to give others his version of what he had learned. This would have been pretty laudable if he was a laptop sharing the facts, but this mission wasn't really about that. This mission was about Leroy trying to prove to both himself and the rest of the world that he was a somebody. It was all about his ego. He had confused knowing about success with being successful. He thought that talking about what he'd learned on his travels would make it all happen for him. Perhaps Leroy isn't really all that bright after all, because he didn't understand that a twenty-year-old man sharing his life wisdom with teenagers may be 'cool', but that, twenty years on, a forty-something bloke in an Ali G tracksuit is not so much cool as creepy.

Leroy had picked up some great friends on his 'journey', many of whom tried to point out that what he was doing wasn't working. Some even attempted to help him pick through the bones of his better ideas and turn them into financial achievements. Unfortunately, Leroy wasn't having any of it. His dream of being a huge success remained a dream. He ploughed on, doing the same thing in the same way, again and again, but over time to smaller, maybe slightly questioning, audiences of young people, who may not have been sure why a middle-aged man was jumping around, extolling the virtues of something that quite clearly had not worked for him. They could see that he wasn't driving a new Ferrari or living in the lap of luxury in some exotic location. They could hear that his language was no longer that of their classroom, that his ideas about young people weren't anything like theirs, and that he had the whiff of desperation about him. None of this endeared him to his audience.

The truth was that, instead of the luxury and life success his so-called strategies were supposed to deliver, he was broke. While his friends had actually acquired the benefits of a life well lived, he was still looking for things to get better. The trouble is, things never seemed to get better. Apparently it was only Leroy who couldn't figure out why. Shame, really, because a laptop would have had it all figured out years ago.

How many more Leroys are there in the world today? Who knows? There are probably millions, and all of them making a similar mistake – misunderstanding their unconscious emotion and interpreting it as if it could only have one meaning. What a blunder! Those emotions could mean anything. There is no easy way of decoding them; all we can be sure of is that they mean something. It's then up to us to be resourceful and try to figure out just what it is trying to tell us.

Psychology informs us that when you feel your gut telling you something it's because your brain has taken in, and processed, tons of information that is somehow relevant to whatever is going on with you at that time. All that mass of data has been painstakingly gathered by your senses and these connections have now come together to help you understand and to navigate you through life. Your subconscious is very clever indeed. But if you do a Leroy and don't even try to interpret the goings on around you, then it might as well not bother. You are designed to be a success, not a failure. Every component in your brain is there for a reason, and that reason is to serve you. Every nerve that carries a message from one part of your body to another is doing it for just one reason – to serve you. So how do you think you're going to feel if you don't make the best use of all that effort? Yes, pretty rubbish, which is probably how Leroy felt when his unconscious was trying desperately to tell him that things were wrong. However, instead of asking a better question, he just attributed that crappy feeling to the fact that his friends were telling him to change. If I still have to spell out the lesson, then you've not been listening. When you get a gut feeling, don't assume you know what it is. Don't assume it's inherently negative – and don't, for goodness' sake, ignore it. Instead, ask a better question, and keep on asking until you feel better. Your gut will tell you when you're on the right track.

Here's how to avoid being Leroy:

1   Potential isn't the same as success. To make your potential materialise, you have to recognise what's getting in the way of you achieving it, even if the biggest barrier is you. You must keep your ego in check, because if it isn't it will stop you dead in your tracks. Instead, you must imagine what your realised potential will look like, sound like and feel like. Then, and only then, can you ask the toughest question of all: 'Is what I'm doing now taking me closer to, or further away from, where I really want to go?'

2   Your future is at risk from disasters of your own making; your current success is no indication of what's to come in your future, nor is your current lack of success. We live in a dynamic world that responds to whatever we do. The more resourceful you allow yourself to be, the more dynamically you'll respond, and the better results you'll end up achieving.

3   Trust your gut — not to tell you what to do, but that it's telling you to investigate further. You can't know what your gut feeling means. It may be that a feeling of dread is trying to tell you not to miss a fabulous opportunity. Equally, a positive gut feeling may be telling you to positively avoid something, and stay in control of your future. The only thing you can be sure of is that you have gut feelings for a reason, and they deserve investigation.

How to avoid dealing with a bad situation badly

WTF just happened to my ability to face tough stuff and deal with it?

These days, being diagnosed with cancer doesn't have to be a death sentence but it still makes most people pause and take stock. I don't want to sound overly gloomy, but if your time might be short anyway, then time suddenly becomes even more precious than it was before you knew you were terminally ill. At least, I'd like to think it would. Yet, even armed with the knowledge that all that can be done has been, and the sands of time are almost gone, some people do the strangest things. Barry was one of them. He knew he had cancer, but kept the diagnosis a secret from everyone, including his family and his colleagues.

'Sod!' One word was all it took to start an avalanche of expletives from Barry. It was how he reacted to stress, and as learning about his disease was about as stressful as it gets, this was his first response here too. Regardless of his fluency in French, Spanish, German and Italian, his sometimes highly inappropriate language got him in trouble. He'd go off like a firework at the drop of a hat, and often joked about his blood pressure being so high that, if it wasn't for his skin, he'd be a fountain. His colleagues were always more concerned about which Barry had turned up for their meeting: the fun, happy Barry who was feeling great and not under pressure, the sulky Barry who'd been called out for his bad behaviour, the genuinely ill Barry who couldn't eat or drink because of the pain, or the frustrated, angry Barry who swore like a trooper and cursed anyone unfortunate enough to be in sight. He was a handful: always a larger-than-life character, first to arrive in the office and last to leave a party. In fact, friends used to joke that Barry had Merlot in his veins, not blood. For a relatively young man, he had a catalogue of stories more exciting and interesting than people twice his age. He had a funny story about everything, could spin a joke about any subject, and oozed bonhomie from every pore – but as entertaining as he was, and as understandable as his response to stress was, this didn't serve him well. However, Barry survived. At home with his wife and family, Barry could be a lovable handful, and at the same time a frightening source of concern. One day he could be full of fun, with apparently not a care in the world, while the next he could be remorseful, moody and defensive. He was irritatingly unpredictable. He could have told his wife what was going on, he could have taken time away from work, and he could have used his considerable creativity and intelligence to deal with a tough situation so that it caused him less stress, not more, but he didn't. He told nobody that he was fighting the disease.

Barry's WTF moment happened when a tsunami of events came crashing down on him. It started with a row one Sunday evening. His wife had had just about enough of him spending almost the whole weekend either working or at the pub, while she ferried their twins between football practice, ballet and a school friend's birthday party. She had no idea he was ill, no idea what he was going through, and so assumed his poor behaviour was just Barry being Barry. However, Barry was actually in such pain and felt so ill that he didn't know what to do with himself. The worse his behaviour became, the worse he felt; he convinced himself there was no point in apologising, as there was nothing he could do about his illness/pain/response. When he 'lost it' at work more than he normally did, his colleagues started losing patience with him. They had no idea that the deterioration was due to anything sinister. Barry could have told them, he could have told everyone, but he didn't. Whenever he behaved badly, he just sloped off and hid for the rest of the day, then pulled himself together and took every new day as it came.

One day, when Barry arrived at the office there were already people in the district manager's office, having a meeting. His boss called him in as soon as he laid eyes on him. The others in the office were the HR person and someone else Barry only vaguely recognised as being from head office. He turned out to be there to help investigate a series of complaints about Barry: not his work, per se, but complaints about his behaviour, the language he was reported to have used, and the implications to the company of some of the reckless statements Barry had made. He'd been accused of being racist and derogatory to others. It looked serious, but Barry was in no mood to deal with them.

Whatever was going on inside Barry's head wasn't serving him well that day. Instead of quietly listening and responding professionally, Barry went on the offensive. He growled an initial response and then gradually turned up the volume as he grew angry. The others in the room didn't appear to want to interrupt, probably allowing Barry to hang himself, but Barry was past caring. As if in a trance of rage, he told them in no uncertain terms why 'people like them with their petty rules and nothing better to do' got in the way of hard-working men and women like him, who got up earlier and went to bed later, doing more work in a week than others could get through in a month, and so it continued until, without warning and in mid-sentence, Barry collapsed.

The rather dull man from head office never did get a chance to do anything about Barry or his outrageous behaviour, because Barry was rushed into hospital. He hasn't been home since, and there's no chance he will ever be coming back to work. By the time his wife reached the hospital, Barry was unresponsive. She had no idea if he could hear her when she told him how sorry she was that they'd fought, or how much she and the twins loved him. She spent the time they had holding his hand and talking to him, even though he couldn't respond.

Everyone at the office was stunned. The 'hit squad' from head office were more annoyed, because they were irritated at having their precious time wasted. Their precious time? It turns out, it was Barry's time that was precious. He'd had a heart attack. With the cancer in so many parts of his body, there was nothing more they could do for him but try to keep him comfortable.

Of course, Barry had known for a while that it had been going on too long for there to be any chance of treatment or recovery but, instead of getting his house in order, confiding in his wife, and making memories in whatever time he had left, he spent it getting angry and fearful at work. What was that all about? What was he thinking? Could he have spent his time better? Could he have dealt with it better than he did? Was he even capable of dealing with something like cancer any better than he did? Who knows? All anyone can do is hope that they do the best job they can with the skills they have, and use whatever time they have as wisely as they can.

Returning to Robert Dilts' hierarchy of thinking levels, cascading downwards from purpose: if you try to talk to someone about an issue at a lower level of the hierarchy while they are actually thinking at a level above it, they won't hear you. Think of it like a set of steps: the nearer to the top you think, the more your thinking influences the levels below. However, try to influence from the bottom upwards and it just won't work.

People in Barry's position often think at the level of values and beliefs (level four), and are apt to say things like 'I'm the kind of person who …', which means that if his co-workers or even his wife talk to him at the level of his behaviours (right near the bottom), then he can't process what they are saying. Beyond knowing what the words mean, he just won't get it. But if you ask him a question at a higher level, say at identity (level five, so just above the level he is thinking) that might go something like, 'What kind of father do you see yourself as, Barry?', this may lead to a response like, 'I don't know … Maybe a caring dad, one who puts his family first.' At this point it is easy to ask a question like: 'Is ignoring a possibly serious illness, and making yourself vulnerable to heart attacks and strokes by getting so het up, being a caring dad? Is that how a caring dad puts his family first?'

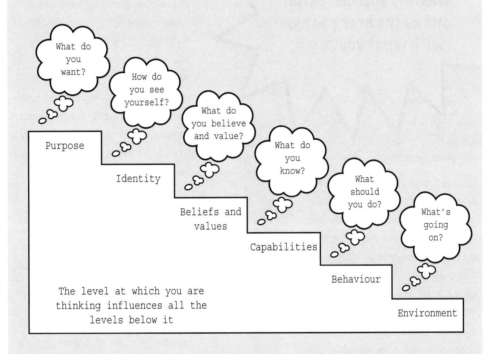

What do you want?

How do you see yourself?

What do you believe and value?

What do you know?

What should you do?

What's going on?

Purpose

Identity

Beliefs and values

Capabilities

Behaviour

Environment

The level at which you are thinking influences all the levels below it

Adapted from Robert Dilts' Neurological Thinking Levels

Here's how to avoid wasting your potential and do the best you can with what you've got:

1 Be realistic: you're going to die one day, that much you can be sure of, but does that day need to be sooner rather than later? You have the power to identify and change any behaviours that put you into a higher risk category. It is valuable to recognise that by doing nothing about them, you are doing something; you are actively saying, 'It's OK for me to die sooner than I have to.' If that is true, then knock yourself out and get on with it because ultimately it is your choice, but if it is not true then, for your own sake, act now.

2 Listen to the people you care about, respect or love; they are most likely to actually care about you and have your best interests at heart. So, if they say 'you're going to kill yourself doing that', don't ignore them. At the very least, ask what it is about your behaviour that's causing them to be concerned about you. The ultimate arrogance is to ignore everyone else's opinion and think that you know best; the ultimate irony is when you drop dead before your time.

3 Be clear about the identity you hold for yourself and whether your behaviours are consistent with it. If you see yourself as being a caring friend, is that what you do? If you call yourself a terrific boss, are you acting like one? If you believe you want to get the most out of life, is that the way you are living?

Tina may not have deserved it, but she was a human doormat and didn't ask particularly good questions, even when she knew she could. Tina was scared of being rejected – by anyone, at any time, and about anything. She sought approval at every turn, and it ended up potentially ruining her life. There are more Tinas in this world than most people realise, which is probably why so many scam-artists succeed in stealing so many identities. The need for approval is normal, but the need for excessive approval certainly isn't. Successful people know how to say no.

'Could you cover for me on Saturday?' Rory asked Tina one day.

'Of course, no problem,' Tina replied.

Tina didn't mean it was no problem. Rory knew she didn't mean it, and the rest of the team knew she didn't mean it, but he was going to accept her answer anyway – after all, someone had to cover the shift and Tina never said no. Tina isn't stupid, but she is silly. She is so concerned with being compliant that she doesn't stop to think what the outcome of that compliance will be. She is the same with everything: a pop-up appears on her social media page that says 'You've won a £500 voucher, just click here for details,' and she clicks, giving away her details to some potential scammer.

Tina was timid, trusting and – to a scammer – a dream 'mark'. Tina is an approval junkie. She wants to be liked, and doesn't want to say no if she can possibly help it. This leads her down some unhealthy paths: such as lending a friend more than she can afford, and then having to borrow money herself from a payday loan company, signing an agreement with huge interest rates that made saying yes to her friend an expensive mistake. The friend didn't pay her back, which meant Tina had to borrow more to pay back what she'd borrowed, plus the interest, and so it went on until her loan was extortionate. By the time her friend did pay her back, Tina was in serious debt. It took her ages to clear, and meant a whole year without a holiday or being able to do anything fun during the summer. Inside Tina was seething, but outwardly she smiled and kept right on seeking approval wherever she went.

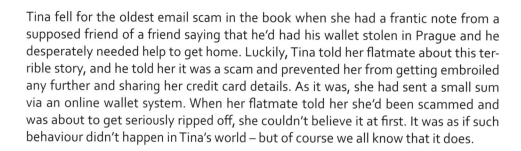

Tina was timid, trusting and – to a scammer – a dream 'mark'. Tina is an approval junkie. She wants to be liked, and doesn't want to say no if she can possibly help it.

Tina fell for the oldest email scam in the book when she had a frantic note from a supposed friend of a friend saying that he'd had his wallet stolen in Prague and he desperately needed help to get home. Luckily, Tina told her flatmate about this terrible story, and he told her it was a scam and prevented her from getting embroiled any further and sharing her credit card details. As it was, she had sent a small sum via an online wallet system. When her flatmate told her she'd been scammed and was about to get seriously ripped off, she couldn't believe it at first. It was as if such behaviour didn't happen in Tina's world – but of course we all know that it does.

It therefore came as no surprise to anyone who knew her that Tina fell for the latest scam, and that this time her credit identity had been seriously damaged. The first she knew about it was an advisory email from her phone company, confirming that her new SIM card had been switched. At first Tina assumed the email had been sent in error, because she didn't know anything about switching a phone SIM card. However, when she went to withdraw some cash from her bank account and found that her balance of over a thousand pounds was now zero, she began to panic. Her panic was well founded.

Apparently a criminal gang had gained access to her basic details – home address, full name and date of birth – and her mobile number. They had used it to contact the phone company and had convinced an operator to believe a made-up sob story, so that the operator overrode the company's basic security systems and authorised a new SIM card for the woman pretending to be Tina.

Tina had been chosen because she lived in a flat with a low-tech set of mail boxes on the wall which could be opened easily. Her mail was intercepted and the new SIM card used to rip off her identity. The scammers knew that people like Tina would use online banking and a two-step method of security, including having codes sent to her mobile, and that, having accessed her mobile account, it wasn't difficult to then access everything about Tina stored on her behalf, wherever that might be. In short, Tina was Tina no more, and she had no way of proving that she wasn't making the many online purchases as the scammers used up her limits on store and credit cards. It was a nightmare unfolding before Tina's trusting eyes.

Fortunately for Tina, she was able to prove that the phone operator was responsible for the problem, and she was given professional support to put her credit history back together. I guess it might have cost the phone company more if she had been the kind of person to take them to court, but it didn't come to that. However, if Tina hadn't been able to prove it wasn't her fault, she would have been left in deep trouble. Apparently these gangs can be very thorough and will scour a person's use of social media to find out their relatives' and pets' names, and anything else that gives them clues to passwords, because they know these words are of massive value: they are keys to unlock a person's identity.

... if Tina hadn't been able to prove it wasn't her fault,
she would have been left in deep trouble.

If Tina had not been able to fix this, it's highly unlikely she could have got a mortgage, approval for a bank loan, or even been able to rent a flat. Her life could have been in ruins, purely because she gave too much of herself away.

Psychologists recognise that some people have an excessive need for approval. Before the advent of social media, this might only have been manifested as a person finding it difficult to say no to any seemingly reasonable request: 'Could you do this little extra job for me?' 'Will you take on this project for us?' 'Can you arrange X or Y?' All of these may be innocuous on their own, but can build into a deep resentment which is not good for the person experiencing it – or the people who end up feeling its backlash. In today's online world these approval-seekers may share more about themselves than is good for anyone, and take on causes that they don't necessarily really believe in. It's still as damaging, and still likely at some point to result in a backlash, as well as also having the potential for that information to be used by the unscrupulous.

Here's how to avoid saying yes when you mean no and the consequences that come with it:

1   Self-protection is a vital component of survival, whereas approval, on the other hand, is a temporary desire that fulfils a need to connect with other people and feel valued. Everyone needs to feel connected and valued — but not at the risk of self-protection. Therefore, before saying yes to anything, be sure that it is something that you really want to do, not something that you are doing for approval.

2   The online world of technology need be no scarier than the real world of loan sharks and huge interest rates. You are not being paranoid if you think that there are people out there who want to get you; there are, and they will if you let them. It's up to you to be aware of what you do and to protect yourself. Don't use passwords that any casual online stalker could figure out easily; don't put financial paperwork into the paper recycling without shredding it if you don't want someone to read it and steal it; and don't allow anyone else to access your mail but you.

3   Think about what you want your online presence to do. If you want to share what you are up to with the world, then have at it, but please be aware of the potential consequences. If you want to separate your business self from your personal self then you have to do more than just have different accounts, because the bad people are not stupid people, and they will find you.

How to avoid 'losing it' during a panic

WTF just happened to my memory and my mind?

Imogen's new associate position as an independent contractor didn't start well at all. Almost anyone stepping into a new opportunity knows they're being judged by just about everyone they meet. Unfortunately, Imogen panicked. Panic is a reaction to fear, and it can happen to everyone. Few people manage panic well, but if you expect to feel fear, and prepare for it, then you stand a chance of not allowing a bout of panic to take hold and take over. Imogen's story is about a woeful lack of preparation and being unprepared for dealing with panic. When that happens it's as if everything you know has been deleted. Your mind goes blank and you can't think.

Oh dear. What a mess Imogen got herself into. 'I'll have to get back to you about that' is never an acceptable response to a question in front of an audience of her peers. Nor is 'I'll dig that out and send it to you afterwards' or 'I don't have the answer to that right now, but I'll let you know.' Imogen was better than that. In her late fifties, she had a wealth of accumulated knowledge and experience in the jet-set worlds of London, Paris and Madrid haute couture, so when an opportunity to join a high-end retail consultancy presented itself it seemed like the perfect fit for her – excuse the pun.

However, it wasn't an easy entry. The door into the consultancy was barred with multiple layers of questioning by phone, face-to-face interviews and then mock customer presentations to a panel of the most senior consultants in the firm. 'We want more than knowledge' was how the senior partner put it. 'We want style, gravitas and that special insight that's hard to define, but when a client sees it they recognise that consultant as being one of ours.' They weren't trying to put her off – far from it. They'd told Imogen from the start that when she'd popped up on their radar they couldn't believe their good fortune, and that they were sure that she would fulfil every criterion for joining.

Lo and behold, they were right. She aced the telephone questionnaire, confidently impressed the interview panel, and did an outstanding job in the mock customer presentation. They told her she had what it took to be one of the best, and as they considered themselves to be the best, she needed to join them. Imogen was delighted. Apart from the prestige of the job, their client list read like the *Who's Who* of the world fashion industry. She was delighted because not only were the clients she'd be dealing with at the very top of their game, but the fees she'd be charging for her time, the first-class air travel and the extended stays in some of the world's finest hotels all added up to a very good deal indeed.

Imogen was not one to count her chickens, but on this occasion she couldn't help herself. Then she received an invitation to the consultancy's annual conference, awards and dinner, which were scheduled for late the following month. As one might imagine, this was no all-you-can-eat buffet and free bar in a Holiday Inn, but a sparkling evening in the heart of London's West End. The day would consist of a 'getting to know you' networking champagne brunch with associates from all over the world, followed by a formal conference until mid-afternoon. After this they'd all be free again to either mingle or take timeout in their luxurious suites, before congregating for a formal dinner and awards ceremony in the ballroom.

When she read all this it sounded amazing – until she got to the bit about the conference agenda. It was to begin with a 'state of the nation' address from the chairman of the firm, a presentation on the year ahead by the head of marketing, and then the remainder of the agenda was given over to formal presentations from new associates. In Imogen's invitation, she was asked to confirm what aspect of continued professional development or special interest she would like to share with her colleagues, and to provide an outline of her twenty-minute speech. At first she was taken aback. Why had no one mentioned this before? What was expected of her? How was she to know how to pitch her speech? These questions, and more, were answered when she plucked up the courage to call her new boss. She told Imogen to 'be herself', choose something that she thought would interest a group of people just like herself, who were as experienced as she was and as interested in the industry as her. That helped, and Imogen got to work preparing her presentation. She wrote the outline and emailed it in as requested. Within twenty-four hours she'd had a reply saying it looked splendid and that everyone was looking forward to it. So that was that. Or was it?

Having now sent in her proposal, which was all about a topic with which she was very familiar, she put it to the back of her mind and got on with the job of being fabulous, something Imogen believed with all her heart she was born to be. Before she knew it, it was the evening prior to the conference. After dinner, she sat down and took an hour or so to put together some slides to support her notes, had a nightcap and then went to bed. The next day, she arrived on time with her slideshow on a thumb drive. She felt fully prepared.

Brunch was a huge success, and all her new colleagues were in high spirits as they sat down for the formal conference. The 'state of the nation' address was so well rehearsed that the speaker's off-the-cuff remarks really did appear natural, and the head of marketing could easily have another career as an inspirational speaker. The supporting graphics each had used were professional, and the best word to describe what Imogen was seeing was 'slick'. Imogen was starting to feel slightly nauseous: nothing to do with the brunch, but as each of the new associates took to the podium for their turn it became obvious that they'd all put a good deal more time and effort into their 'turn in the spotlight' than she had. Every minute closer to her slot saw her mouth getting just that bit drier and her mind racing that little bit faster. She was giddy with fear, angry with herself for missing an obvious opportunity to shine, and growing in certainty that when she got up to speak it would be her undoing. Unfortunately, she was right. It was.

Imogen was not so much fabulous and flawless as befuddled and forlorn. She panicked. Her slides were so obviously amateurish that she found herself apologising for them with each click of her hand-held pointer. More panic. She kept on losing her place and having to refer to her notes, and the warmth with which she had been welcomed onto the podium was fast cooling. She could feel it, they could feel it, and they all knew that the senior people in the room could feel it too – her massive palpable level of panic, and that was never going to lead to a happy ending.

> She wasn't what they had expected, and that wasn't good. When the time came for her Q&A session, things turned ugly. Gone were the smiles and gushing bonhomie so freely flowing at brunch, and in their place was an atmosphere thick with tension.

If Imogen was thinking WTF? then the others in the room were probably thinking it too. She wasn't what they had expected, and that wasn't good. When the time came for her Q&A session, things turned ugly. Gone were the smiles and gushing bonhomie so freely flowing at brunch, and in their place was an atmosphere thick with tension. The pack had sensed an imposter in its midst, one that was cut down further with every question Imogen either failed to answer or answered incompletely. The smell of blood in the air caused the pack to circle their prey, getting closer each time a new question lashed out and caught poor Imogen unawares. She was saved by the bell – at least temporarily. Her twenty minutes was up and she was able to return to her place.

Dinner was a nightmare. People were outwardly polite to her, but no one took the time to build a relationship with her. It was as if they already knew she was beyond help and, truth be told, she was. Just two days after the conference she received a letter from the chairman thanking her for her time and for attending the conference, and hoping a suitable project would come along that 'will provide an opportunity for you to work with us'. It was a polite way of saying 'You've wasted our time and we won't waste yours any more, so this is goodbye.' She knew there would never be a suitable project. She returned her business cards unopened and didn't bother including a note. There was no need; everyone knew what had happened, and there was nothing left to say.

Psychology tells us that people create their own realities; we filter the information around us and unconsciously pick from it those things that match patterns we already recognise, patterns we don't know we have. If your patterns include ways to deal with panic and strategies to handle difficult situations then you will notice them, and respond accordingly. Without those patterns, there's nothing for us to base a response on. A poor strategy to deal with panic will make your mind go blank. Even basic things that in other circumstances would come straight to your mind just disappear.

Here's how to avoid looking like you've lost it:

1 Get over the fact that you are being judged every moment of every day. Your partner will judge you, your kids will judge you, your co-workers will judge you, and as sure as eggs are eggs your boss will judge you too. So no matter how good you were yesterday, no matter how great your CV looks, you had better perform today, right here, right now.

2 People lie. People who want something from you lie even more. So when they tell you you're the best thing since sliced bread, you had better take it with a pinch of salt or you are setting yourself up to be sucker-punched. As soon as you don't give them what they want, they will find your weak spot and they will use it. If they don't, then consider it a bonus. It is not an excuse for you to be unprepared.

3 Nothing is ever over, even when the fat lady appears to have sung her last note. You may have been told you are wonderful, you may have done a good job, you may look the part and say all the right things – but if you don't demonstrate the quality and performance that someone is expecting, then you will pay the price. There is no reason for you to forget who you are and what you know, except if you lose concentration because you lack preparation and practice. No performer is 'brilliant' the first time out; practice isn't just about memory, it's about expectation and the uncovering of tiny distinctions that other people don't see. The more familiar you become with whatever you need to demonstrate, the more comfortable and confident you will become, and the more you will recognise the appropriateness of whatever support material you use. You will get it right first time, every time, because it won't really be your first time; professionals make sure of that.

Whoever said ignorance was bliss clearly hadn't thought through the consequences, something that Luca realised too late.

Before you begin reading, a word of warning: the subject matter of this section is suicide. If you have been affected by anything related to this subject, I strongly advise you ensure that you are ready to review the subject dispassionately and objectively. If not, please skip this one and move on to the next.

Ignorance and a lack of awareness of your own behaviours is not only deeply wounding for people around you, but it will eventually bite you on the backside too. Since the dawn of civilisation, human beings have believed that our behaviours accumulate and, like the notion of karma, are at some point accounted for. The ancient Egyptians painted intricate murals of an imagined death ceremony where a person's life actions, represented by their heart, are weighed against the universal measure of goodness known as *maat*, represented by a feather, and if the heart weighed heavier than the feather, a future in the underworld awaited them. On the other hand, if the heart weighed the same as the feather, this indicated that you had lived a life of goodness and were free to continue onwards and upwards. Buddhist beliefs about reincarnation and karma have a different approach but similar foundations: if you have failed to learn something in this life, you must come back and experience a life that teaches it to you, and that life may not be as pleasant as this one, but if you have learned lessons and are ready to learn more, your new life may be pleasant enough to allow that to happen. Most religious traditions have similar value constructs that urge people to be aware of what they are doing because it will benefit them, as well as those around them, but you don't need to share any religious belief to recognise that this is simply common sense.

Luca had no idea what was going on around him. He was self-centred, thick-skinned and emotionally deficient – he didn't deserve the love his wife gave him. There's little stigma attached to divorce these days. But Luca's loss was far greater, his pain more acute, and it all happened without him having any idea there was a problem, or at least that the problem was as acute as it proved to be.

The moment you hear that someone close to you has taken their own life is impossible to forget. Such was the experience of Luca and his children when the police officer delivered the devastating news. His wife Maria had apparently left for work as normal, but never arrived. Her boss, assuming she had a good reason for her absence and would fill him in later, didn't raise the alarm. It wouldn't be the first time she had forgotten to tell him about a client appointment, and her diary was rarely up to date, so there were no clues to suggest a problem. When Luca picked up the children from school, however, he was surprised to see her car on the drive. Discovering she wasn't home, he checked her car. The engine was cold, which told him she hadn't recently come home; her phone wasn't in the car, and he'd been calling her since he got home so he began to panic. He found the phone vibrating in her bag which was in her wardrobe and, after confirming she hadn't been at work, he called the police.

Sadly, earlier that day they had found a dead woman slumped on a bench in the village cemetery. With no identification on her and no record of her fingerprints on file, the police had no way of knowing who she was. Luca's call and the photograph he emailed the police from his phone gave them immediate confirmation. It was Maria. Apparently she had gone to the cemetery almost as soon as her husband and children had left on the school run. She had overdosed. As far as the police could tell, she took the overdose while sitting on the bench. The autopsy confirmed that she had taken a large volume of prescription painkillers and antidepressants – far more than she should have been able to access. The police later assumed she had been hoarding these pills from regular prescriptions.

Luca's terrible WTF moment happened not when he heard of her suicide, but later, when he faced the truth that his supposedly loving wife and caring mother of their children had been planning this for months. The realisation that this was no spur-of-the-moment act made it much worse. The more he analysed their life together, the more convinced he became that this devastating event was actually his fault. Of course, it wasn't, but it was hard for him to believe anything else; hard for him not to torture himself; and hard for him to do anything but take one breath after the next.

He received some counselling to help him come to terms with her death, and this led him to believe that Maria had been suffering from a psychological condition, and that she was as ill when she killed herself as a person might be with any comparable physical disease. The doctor was at pains to stress that not being able to see an illness made it no less real. Even so, Luca could not shake the idea that, whatever the condition was, it had been his fault. That's hard.

It was this information that went through Luca's mind when he had his 'moment'. Questions raced through his thoughts: what kind of husband was I not to notice? Why didn't Maria feel able to share with me that she wasn't feeling well? What must she have been feeling when going through this alone? And of course the big one: could I have saved her if I had done something differently? These are terrible questions, because they can't be answered. The best Luca could do was make up an answer but then, because he knew it was made up, he didn't believe it. He concluded that there was no point in asking questions he couldn't answer. It didn't help him because every road led back to his growing conviction that it was his fault. That's even harder.

Hang on, you might say. You might ask: how could Luca be self-centred, thick-skinned and emotionally deficient if he was being a diligent dad and doing the school run on the day Maria died?

The answer is that he was so self-obsessed that he never saw anything wrong with his behaviour. As far as he was concerned, the decisions he made, the direction he gave his family and the 'support' he gave his wife were exemplary. However, on closer inspection he wasn't as angelic as he made out; he was controlling, dismissive of other people's opinions, unaware of other people's feelings. He appeared to have little or no conscience when someone else got hurt or was upset, if they were getting in the way of Luca getting what he wanted – and worst of all, he did it all with a smile. He didn't shout and wasn't angry; he just did whatever he had to do to get what he wanted. Early in their marriage Maria had tried arguing with him, getting upset with him, withholding sex from him, and even complaining to his parents about him, but nothing seemed to bother Luca. He would smile, tell her that she had a point, but on this occasion it had to be his way or no way, and so it went on. After reflecting on what had really happened, and finally admitting to himself what he had been like and how he had behaved to his family, Luca came to the conclusion that he might have worn Maria down until she had nowhere to go and she felt that suicide was the only option left open to her. As a WTF moment, that's about as hard as it gets.

It is by no means certain that Luca was right in blaming himself; but being told this didn't make it any easier for him. He had to live with the situation and had to do his best, if not for himself, then for their children.

Here's how to avoid painful ignorance:

1 Look around and see how the people closest to you react to you. Are they at ease and relaxed, do they meet your eye, and do they carry on with whatever they were doing when you walk into the room? If you sense any tension, a lack of eye contact or any indication that people are avoiding you, then you need to pay attention. You need to start asking what you are doing to cause this. Notice that I said what *you* are doing, and not what *their* problem is: this is your problem, your behaviour and your state of mind that's causing other people to respond negatively to you. It's therefore up to you to figure out what you are doing and change it.

2 Listen to how you talk to other people. Are you respectful, are you patient, are you at pains to understand what they mean, what their intention is, and if you are achieving your outcome? If you hear yourself being less than respectful, then you have a problem. *You* have a problem, not anyone else. It's not someone else's job to put up with your lack of communication skills, make allowances for you, or agree with you when they don't. If you force people to agree with you, then you can be sure that they're only paying lip service and at the first opportunity they will find a way around it.

3 Recognise that you are not the only person in the world with emotions. Everybody has emotions, everyone has needs and desires, and everyone wants to satisfy them. However, if you put your emotional needs before other people's, then you will pay the price. If you are so out of touch with other people's emotions that you don't realise you are subjugating theirs in order to fulfil your own, then you will hurt them. If you hurt them badly enough, they will find a way to hurt you too.

How to avoid losing your friends

WTF just happened to the people who are supposed to care about me?

Everyone has an image of themselves, and it's healthy for that image to be a good one. However, if the image in a person's mind bears no resemblance to the way they are really perceived by the rest of the world, then it will become a problem. The same is true with our beliefs about other people, because if we think we are someone's friend, but they don't share that view, there's bound to be a problem. Such was the case with Neil. You see, Neil thought he had lots of friends. Neil thought 'people love me'. Neil was wrong. We all know a Neil, don't we? The bloke who thinks he's God's gift to the opposite sex? He's the one who can't pass a mirror without looking in it just to remind himself how fabulous he is. You must know someone like that, eh? Relax, I know you probably look in the mirror too, but that doesn't mean you are anything like Neil. Unfortunately for him, his rather warped image of himself caused him to behave in ways that were ultimately very damaging. His story should act as a warning for all of us to just check in once in a while to make sure that what we think about ourselves is at least shared by one other person!

The term 'friend' is confusing. Here's how friendship worked before social media usurped the term 'friend': young people met other young people at school and those friends from school were accidental. If you'd gone to a different school or been born a couple of years before or after, your friends from school would be different. I recall attending a reunion at my alma mater a few years ago, and after accepting a welcome drink and wandering around for five minutes, wondered if I'd come to the right school. I knew I'd gone there and that I was in the right location, but where were all my old mates? I didn't recognise anyone, for the simple reason that most were a decade or so younger than me. I might as well have been a random guest at a corporate event; at least then I'd have expected to know no one.

Your old schoolmates may feel like bosom buddies, but in actual fact are as random as it gets, which explains why most of them have so little in common with you now. They are probably as freaked out that you all hung out together as you are. Maybe you have enough in common with one or two to still want to mix with them, but don't hold your breath. Old schoolmates aren't mates, really; they were just convenient at the time, they just happened to be there. Friends you made at uni, college, your apprenticeship or job training have a better chance of being genuine friends. At least you share a common interest; even so, you still didn't choose them. The same issue of age applies, so does course and educational establishment or place of work. Random, random, random.

By the time you get into work you now have a set of colleagues and you have only one big thing in common: work. They are not friends; you didn't choose them nor they you. You haven't done anything to match their profiles against your own or consider their core values against yours. By 'profiles' I don't mean the few lines a person shares on social media sites; I'm talking about the real you: your likes and loves, needs and desires, everything about you. That's the profile that needs to overlap for people to become real friends, and that rarely happens by meeting random people at work. You will have more success finding better matches by walking down the high street chatting to strangers. Seriously, you would, because of your unconscious filtering of information. Your brain is like a super-computer in your head, tossing out data that's useless and hanging on to other stuff it thinks might be useful. If you walk around enough and talk to enough people, eventually you'll meet someone you like, and that you like for a good reason, not just because they're there.

Research in the United States into workplace romance tells us that millions of people meet their spouse at work, often after having a sexy secretive affair.[*] It's also a meeting that causes many to then meet a divorce lawyer. It's beyond me why anyone would be surprised that marrying someone they meet because someone else has put them in close proximity would result in anything else but a growing realisation that they don't have much in common, outside of work and a bunch of trivial connections, which are made to feel more important than they are because of good old-fashioned sexual chemistry. Unfortunately, that wears off eventually and all that's left is confusion: 'How the heck did we get here?' The internet looked for a while like it was going to help build better intimate relationships and deeper friendships, and to be fair it has helped a little, but nothing is as powerful as meeting plenty of people in situations that support a good match. It can't be a coincidence that it's suggested people who meet in church tend to divorce less often than others, probably because they already share similar values.[†] Perhaps the same is true for those who meet at chess clubs or at am-dram groups. The more people have in common, the better; they may end up becoming real friends, then best friends, and if that gets mixed in with a good dose of sexual chemistry, a long and happy relationship might be more likely.

It's definitely going to stand a better chance than picking from the severely limited gene pool of the office. It's not rocket science, yet people like Neil think they can get through life without making an effort to find someone special. People like Neil allow themselves to believe that superficial acquaintances care about them more than

---

[*] According to the likes of Maureen S. Binetti, 'Romance in the Workplace: When "Love" Becomes Litigation', *Hofstra Labor and Employment Law Journal,* (2007) 25(1): 153–172 and Nolan C. Lickey, Gregory R. Berry and Karen S. Whelan-Berry, 'Responding to Workplace Romance: A Proactive and Pragmatic Approach', *The Journal of Business Inquiry,* (2009) 8(1): 100–119. Available at: https://www.uvu.edu/woodbury/docs/respondingtoworkplaceromance.pdf.

[†] According to Bradley Wright in *Christians Are Hate-Filled Hypocrites … and Other Lies You've Been Told* (Bloomington, MN: Bethany House Publishers, 2010), couples who are active in their faith are much less likely to divorce. Catholic couples are 31% less likely to divorce; Protestant couples 35% less likely; and Jewish couples 97% less likely.

they really do, and that it takes no effort to form or maintain a friendship. That's why people like Neil turn around one day and have their WTF moment as they realise that no one in their life cares very much about them at all. Sad, really, but there you go. You get out what you're prepared to put in, so if you put no effort into making good friendships and maintaining them, intimate or otherwise, this can only lead to one conclusion: one day you will find you are on your own, you have no support, and no one to hold your frightened little hand. It's a scary world and there'll be a time when we all need someone special, so if you are not doing it already, now would be a good time to start.

> Neil got his just desserts by giving the people whose 'rules' he'd broken the ammunition to shoot him with.

The sad fact is, everyone turned on Neil after he was caught 'cooking the books'. Every person he had ever taken for granted in that office seized the opportunity to hit him where it hurt. Every woman he'd pretended to be interested in, whether he'd actually slept with her or not, made sure they avoided any opportunity to help, and his boss (who'd put up with Neil's schmoozing while knowing full well what went on when his back was turned) wasn't going to miss this chance to nail him good and proper. Neil got his just desserts by giving the people whose 'rules' he'd broken the ammunition to shoot him with. He was in sales, and part of his job was to foster relationships with buyers and solicit orders. The sales teams and their team leaders were rewarded with bonuses for reaching individual sales targets and Neil's team was far and away the highest-achieving team, with most of those sales registered to Neil himself, and it was this consistent overachievement that caused questions to be asked. No one could be that good, not even Neil. He was already an outsider, so no one was going to side with him and come to his rescue.

The records system was supposedly tamper-proof, but head of security Dave found evidence that it might be being manipulated. Without corroborated evidence, Dave would never be able to accuse Neil, let alone prove that he was responsible. However, far from being reluctant, Neil's co-workers and even his team had come forward to confirm that they suspected what Dave had come to investigate. It didn't take long for Dave to conclude that Neil was responsible for manipulating sales figures and falsifying sales reports. This was a serious situation: Neil could easily have been prosecuted. The least he could have expected was to be fired, yet when confronted with the accusations, Neil was robust in his own defence. Stupidly, he claimed as his evidence the support of his 'friends'.

That didn't go well. To say Neil was cocky when confronted might be an understatement. Imagine being Dave and hearing this:

Look, Dave, I hope it's OK to call you Dave, or is it David? No matter; all this is a mistake, there's been no over-reporting of sales by my team, and by that of course I mean me — 'team Neil', yeah! My sales are always way ahead of everyone; I'm a popular guy — what can I say? Just ask around, they'll all tell you there's no way I'd do anything like fixing the numbers. It must be a glitch, because I don't need to cheat the system. I'm a winner; they know it, Charlie knows it and so do our clients, which is why they buy from me personally and don't just order randomly from the net. All those sales are legit, so you need to go and look somewhere else to meet your own targets, Mr Dave; there's nothing to see here.

At some level it's easy to feel sorry for him; he just didn't see it coming. No one came to his defence, no one wanted to help him even if they could. He was, quite simply, hung out to dry. In the end he was lucky as he wasn't prosecuted for fraud, but he did get fired. Unfortunately, he appears not to have learned anything from the experience. He's bitter that no one stood up for him, he's shouted about his innocence (although there's no real doubt of his guilt), and this won't do him any favours. So, at another level it's pitiful because with a simple raising of awareness and the asking of a few questions he could have avoided it all.

It is clear how social norms operate; they are an often unspoken set of expectations to which a group conforms. There is a sense of certainty that comes from behaving 'correctly' which feels good. Feeling good is easily confused with somebody causing you to feel good. Attribution theory explains how easy it is for a person to link an emotion with a person or event so strongly that a belief is born; a belief that one is the cause of the other, that one cannot happen without the other, and that if one goes then the other must too. Reality is nothing like that at all. Relationships that last and are good for all parties happen when beliefs are accepted, values are shared and a common goal is acknowledged. If beliefs are not understood or accepted, then meanings will be attributed to behaviour based on nothing but imagination. If values are not shared, then behaviours that appear to be in conflict to another's values will be perceived as an attack. If people who work together don't have a shared goal, then by definition they will have goals that potentially work against each other.

Here's how to avoid being left out in the cold:

1   Everyone needs friends. We don't need many, but we do all need some. Friends are people you can trust, which means they have to be consistent and reliable in their connection with you. They must therefore share some aspects of your life that go beyond work, or when the day comes that you go your way and they go theirs and the work goes, they will be gone forever. You need to respect them, and they you, because you share important values and beliefs, or the moment something comes along to challenge your friendship it will be gone. They need to feel close to you, which means they share things with you in the belief that what they tell you stays with you, but if that level of intimacy isn't achieved or is faked, as soon as they realise it the friendship is gone. Finally, they need to know that you are in the friendship as much for what you can give as for what you can gain, and you need to feel that too. If you don't, that friendship will be gone.

2   Don't mistake fear for friendship. It can happen anywhere, not just at work: people appear to become your friends because they fear that if they are not, they will be in danger; in danger of being left out of a group, in danger of being singled out and picked on, in danger of being left out of gossip, or the unspecified danger of a feeling that just seems to push a person into 'sucking up' to someone who, in other circumstances, they might despise.

3   Be the friend you want to have. Instead of looking for people to be your friend, seek instead to behave in a way that demonstrates you are already a friend to them. Friendship does not happen because a person presses a button on a mobile device to 'accept' you; it happens because a person feels drawn to you for good reasons. You may share values, you may share some interests, you stimulate each other, and, most of all, you trust each other.

How to avoid putting up with unhappiness

WTF just happened to my personal standards?

Hopefully we will all grow old. When we get there, wouldn't it be nice to be able to look back over a life well spent, a life of love, and a life with some great memories rather than regrets? If that's going to happen, then we must have standards when it comes to relationships. Standards lead to expectations, and expectations lead to the results you achieve. She may be getting on a bit now, but Daphne had it all: great friendships, a great career, and what she thought was a great relationship. Where did it all go? It vanished because of something she believed about herself and her standards. Ever wondered what happened to the old woman with the shopping trolley full of empty tin cans and scraps of material? Could the same ever happen to you? No matter how secure any of us feel, we can't know what is around the corner. All we can do is hope that our reserves, both financial and emotional, are enough to keep us out of the gutter.

She may have been on the planet a few more years than you or I, but in her day the world was much as it is today except that the shops all closed on Sundays, the supermarket didn't deliver, Christmas presents were bought months in advance by going to the shops, January sales actually happened in January and you had to be there to buy, and the only hand-held communication devices were on *Star Trek*. Apart from that kind of thing, the big things in life were the same as they are today: happiness came from sharing life with someone you loved and who loved you back, by having a meaningful purpose, and a group of friends, and a supportive family, who you can depend on and who can depend on you.

Daphne was tall for her age. At almost 5 foot 10, fifteen-year-old Daphne could pass for a girl five years her senior. She attracted longing glances from young men with slicked-back hair and their first set of wheels who assumed she was a fully fledged adult. She entered – and won – a local beauty parade, the prize for which was dinner for two at the best restaurant in the city. It was two days after her sixteenth birthday when the letter arrived with the prize confirmation, and it was the best present she'd had. The economy was still recovering from the ravages of a world war, and her parents hadn't changed their eating habits yet from the days of rationing. So the idea of eating whatever she wanted in a smart restaurant was on the one hand enticing, and on the other a little scary. She had no idea how to behave in a restaurant and didn't want to look silly by using the wrong fork, or look at the menu and not understand what was on offer. Still, it was a fabulous prize, and one she was going to savour. There was one big problem, however: who to take. As much as she'd had lots of attention, and although her mum would blow a gasket if she knew, she'd done her fair share of kissing behind the bike sheds, but she didn't have a boyfriend. Back then, a boyfriend was an even bigger deal than it is now. Girls weren't expected to flit from one boyfriend to another, but to choose wisely early on and then stick with him.

It didn't take Daphne too much thought. She'd had her eye on a boy for a while now. He was a little shy and didn't hang around with a gang of stupid friends. Instead, he always seemed to be working: either helping with fizzy pop deliveries, labouring at the brick factory, or covering the late shift at the beer bottling plant. Yet every time she saw him at the milk bar he caught her eye and smiled. His name was Richard and he was cute. She wanted him to be her date, but how could she ask him without looking too keen? It was a dilemma then (as it is now), but after thinking about it for a while, Daphne made a decision.

She didn't know it at the time, but this decision was the start of her WTF moment, even though that moment wouldn't happen for many years. Her decision was pivotal because it changed the way she thought about herself, and it changed the way she believed in herself and how she should interact with people. It changed things because other girls of her age might have had a parent make the introduction and invitation, probably via the parents of the boy receiving the invitation – after all, this wasn't a date at the local cinema but a high-profile invitation to the city's finest restaurant as a follow-up to the city-wide beauty competition. Daphne was the reigning queen, and as such should have expected the press to take an interest. Her dinner was not going to be a private, intimate affair; the restaurant giving it away had demanded they get their fair share of promotional coverage, so the presence of cameras should not have been a surprise to anyone. They were to Daphne.

She didn't tell her parents when the letter arrived, but kept it in her bottom drawer in her bedroom until she was ready to make an invitation herself. She gathered up her courage and, letter in hand, sat in the milk bar that Saturday morning, hoping that Richard wouldn't be working. He wasn't; he walked through the door and smiled at her. Then came that moment after which her life would never be the same again. What kind of girl would stand up, call a boy over, and ask him to join her? Today, probably any girl; back then, not so many. By calling him over and making the first move, and not for just any first date but dinner at a restaurant neither of them could afford, she stood out from the crowd; she put herself into a unique category, a set of one. There wasn't anyone like her that she knew of, and this uniqueness was to shape the rest of her life. She became a law unto herself, setting her personal standards, living up or down to them, and being pleased with the result. Pleased, that is, until it dawned on her that setting her own standards with no regard to the rest of the world meant a mismatch between her expectations and those of everyone else.

However, at the beginning it didn't matter; it all seemed to be good. She invited Richard and they had a fabulous dinner, their pictures were in the paper, and all her friends, and his, were in awe of this new glamorous couple. They fell in love and pledged allegiance to each other. Then Richard was called to do National Service, conscripted for eighteen months and, after basic training, whisked away overseas. In those days there was no texting, WhatsApp or internet to keep in touch. They were apart for a year and a half, during which time Daphne set her own standards of behaviour. She wasn't faithful to Richard; in fact, having made the decision that Richard would be the boy she would marry, she used the time to 'enjoy herself' without any need to concern herself with the depth of any fleeting relationship.

Richard sensed something had changed when he returned. Daphne seemed to have grown up even faster than he had. While he'd been scared out of his wits, handling live firearms that'd forced him into manhood, he chose not to think about what Daphne might have been doing to have made the transition from cute girl into knowing young woman. They married and had a baby girl, but all was not well – even though it should have been.

Daphne used her confidence to become the first woman of her age in the city to set up her own business. Her first shop was successful and soon there was a second and then a third. She employed staff, had her own accountant, and had the money to visit the new best restaurants in the city, drink champagne and throw wild parties regularly. It wasn't a world Richard was used to, or comfortable with. He may well have been one of the first house husbands of his era, giving Daphne the space and time to behave consistently with her own standards. Meanwhile, other people muttered between themselves about her behaviour – not to her face, mind you, because she had fast become known for having a quick temper. It wasn't long before Daphne met a much younger version of Richard, one who accepted her wild ways without censure and who made all the right noises about making her life better. Within months she left Richard and her daughter for a new life.

Fast-forward twenty years. Daphne and her new husband hadn't done well. Her shops were gone, as were any savings. They lived from week to week. Daphne had developed a severe health issue that prevented her from working, and it was up to her husband to provide. He had no trade or profession, as the years when he should have been training had been spent partying with her. Now he struggled to hold down a job of any kind. They lived in a rented flat above a pub, where he managed to secure a part-time job behind the bar in the evenings. Cliché or not, he fell for a busty barmaid, drank his 'tips' every night, and kept away from Daphne as much as possible. One night, Daphne arrived home early from visiting her mother, and caught him in the marital bed with the busty barmaid.

This was Daphne's 'WTF just happened?' moment. In a split second she realised that her own life was reflecting her personal standards. She had no real friends, she had no career to fall back on and she had no relationship. The really sad thing is that Daphne never recovered. She didn't leave him, as she had nowhere to go. She put up with his pleading and promises to give up booze and womanising, knowing perfectly well that it would only end when he was too old, too ugly or too dead to do it any more. Now in her twilight years, she lives in sheltered accommodation with only regrets to keep her company, and a shopping trolley that she wheels around, collecting stuff that may be useful one day. She makes the best of things, but can't escape the fact that she wasn't a victim of life but the victim of living to her own standards.

There is no happy ending if your standards don't allow for one.

The psychology of personal relationships is not as complicated as it's sometimes made out to be. Everybody needs to be sure about the person they give their heart to, and at the same time they need to be excited and challenged by them. They need to see themselves as a pair while at the same time be supported in having an identity of their own. The trouble is, if a person gets so deep into a relationship that they find it hard to climb back out, they will find ways to make it feel like it's working. They 'make up' things to be certain about, and allow negative stimulation to meet their need for excitement. Then they pretend that they're still connected, even though any real connection may have dissipated years ago, and they fool themselves that they're happy with the identity they've created for themselves, even though in their heart they know they hate it.

Here's how to avoid lowering your standards:

1   It may be hackneyed, but I'm saying it anyway: start with your own end in mind. Set your own standards, not by the minimum you can get away with, but by what you'd like to have happen to you. Life will put all manner of barriers in the way of personal happiness, but it's madness to put barriers of your own making in your way by setting personal standards that do not serve you well. If you want a future aimlessly pushing a shopping trolley around and collecting empty tin cans, then set unattainable standards, knowing that you will fail, but if that's not what you want then start getting realistic now; don't wait.

2   If you make a mistake and behave in a way that doesn't meet your own standards, admit it. Acknowledge it and change your behaviour to meet the standards you want for yourself. Don't lower your standards to match your own poor behaviour, because if you do you will live to regret it.

3   Step back and look at yourself. Reflect on the way you are behaving and the standards you are keeping. Ask yourself if these standards reflect the way you want to live and the life you want to lead. Ask yourself if living to these standards is more or less likely to take you in the direction you want to go.

How to avoid saying 'what if' and 'if only'

WTF just happened to my big plans?

Reece had a big shock when it dawned on him that he had become his own worst enemy. Everyone has potential. Some have more of it than others, and some people waste their potential, and wake up one day asking themselves, 'WTF just happened to me?' Beanie hat, rat's tails, hipster beard, faded tour T-shirt and designer ripped jeans that actually came from the market – Reece thought he was cool. Flat broke, in a dead-end job with no plans to do anything about it, but in his own mind he was cool. At least that's what he allowed himself to think for a while. That is, until he compared himself to someone he'd thought beneath him – and found himself wanting. It wasn't a good feeling. Not a good feeling at all.

Reece was going to take the world by storm: not for him a life of being a 'worker bee' buzzing from job to job and not getting anywhere while fat cats lived off the spoils of his labour. Oh no, Reece was going to show them all that there was another way, a better way: the Reece way. Fast-forward to a decade later: by then he worked in the IT department of a City bank, cycled to work every morning, ate his lunch from a plastic container, and then cycled home, along with thousands of other Londoners.

Reece should have graduated from university with a first. His degree should have opened the door to being a high-earner, and should have set his life on the course he'd set his heart on, but it didn't. He had plans to travel the world before he settled down, and knew to the penny how much it was going to cost him, so he should have saved some money when he started earning, but he didn't save and he didn't go travelling. He promised himself that he wouldn't be one of those people caught in a rent trap, and that he was going to do whatever it took to secure a mortgage and buy his own home. But something happened. Despite his terrific plans, in the end he didn't put enough cash together to secure a deposit even for the cheapest deals available, and ten years on he still lived in a rented flat. Worse still, he shared the flat with a bloke he'd advertised for, who rented the spare room.

The facts are that, in his hubris, Reece borrowed more than he could reasonably pay back in this lifetime or the next. He ran up credit card debts until there was nowhere else to run, and lived those ten years as if he would never have to pay his debts. But what had he to show for it? Supposedly, every loan was intended to take him closer to achieving his goals, but instead the cash slipped through his fingers like grains of sand. He had borrowed money so that he could go out and enjoy himself. His big plans went by the board because he lived 'in the moment' and tried not to think of the future. He'd read a book that told him that the most successful people in the world didn't allow themselves to be distracted by what had happened in the past, or what might happen in the future, but who made the most they could of now. It was a philosophy he had both taken to heart and interpreted badly, as there's no way anyone could possibly describe Reece as successful. He was self-indulgent and arrogant with it. His last notion before his WTF moment was to change his life by leaving the country and taking his 'expertise' where he would be more appreciated. Quite where that might have been, and what exactly his expertise was was anyone's guess.

His moment of clarity happened the morning his bike had a puncture and he was forced to take the Tube to work. Station repairs meant that he had to change at Oxford Circus and endure the queues to get on the Tube to Liverpool Street. People tend to try not to look at each other on the London Tube; it's a way of maintaining your own personal space when you don't actually have any, but on this occasion Reece could feel someone's eyes boring into him, eventually forcing him to look up. He'd prepared a pithy comeback in his head, as he expected the only reason someone would be staring at him would be aggressive, but was stopped in his tracks when he recognised who it was.

'Hello mate, I thought it was you underneath all that beardy stuff! How are you? Long time, no see.'

For a second, Reece found it hard to reconcile the Pete he'd known at university with the Pete standing in front of him now. That Pete had been that northerner who spoke with an accent that southerners like Reece found hard to decipher, but this Pete sounded like a 1950s BBC announcer, and looked sharp, very sharp indeed. This is how their conversation went:

Reece: 'Yo, Pete! Good to see you, my man. How's things with you?'

Pete: 'Great, thanks. Goodness, it must be at least ten years?'

Reece: 'Yeah, it must be.'

Pete: 'You're on the way to work?'

Reece: 'Yeah, in the City, you know, IT and all that … you too?'

Pete: 'Oh, er, no, but I am on my way to the City, though. Liverpool Street, and you?'

Reece: 'Yeah, that's my stop too …'

They chatted all the way, but Reece had known the moment he saw Pete that this was his 'WTF just happened to all my own big plans?' moment; he could see, and sense, that Pete was in a very different place in life, and it was probably a place that Reece wished he'd reached too. Pete wasn't on the Tube because his bike was broken, but probably only because it was quicker than trying to get through London in a limo. The more they talked, the more Reece realised that he had had just as many opportunities as Pete, but had made different choices. Pete's degree was actually only a 2:2, while Reece had got a 2:1, so clearly it wasn't a qualification that had made the difference. However, something had.

Pete had worked behind a bar every night and as a security marshal at a big London entertainment venue to save every penny and travel the world, just like Reece had wanted to (but never actually got around to). During his travels Pete had used his education to get temporary jobs along the way. One of these had led to an opportunity: a company in South America wanted representation in the UK and help in raising finance, and having met Pete they became convinced that a bright young man like him was just who they were looking for. On his return to the UK, Pete had duly gone about doing what they'd asked, during which he'd met a number of people involved in private equity. To cut a long story short, he'd been offered a job, had done well, and now represented the company with a number of their big investments. He spent most of his time visiting clients at their various locations around the world. Pete didn't have to tell Reece that the travel was all first class or that the hotels he stayed in were five-star; it just seemed to go with the territory. Pete now lived in a modest house by a golf course near Oxford, but he also had a small apartment on the Thames that he'd been able to snap up during the financial crash. As they say in parts of London, the boy done good. Reece didn't begrudge Pete his life of high finance and luxury, but for the first time in his life he stopped making excuses for himself and realised that what had happened in his life was his own responsibility. 'What ifs' and 'if onlys' can happen at any time and at any age. Maybe Reece still has time to put it right, but only time (and Reece's own actions) can change anything. The things that we believe about ourselves are the things we make come true; we either, like Pete, believe that we can or, like Reece, get lulled into believing that we can't.

> The things that we believe about ourselves are the things we make come true; we either, like Pete, believe that we can or, like Reece, get lulled into believing that we can't.

Psychologists call the unconscious discomfort we feel when conflicting ideas, beliefs or values collide cognitive dissonance. Like when a person knows that something is bad for them but does it anyway; they find excuses for the bad thing so that they can keep on doing it. The drinker who knows that one pint in the pub will always lead to more, and that they really shouldn't, will find an excuse, any excuse, to continue drinking – 'just one more' ... 'you can't drink alone' ... 'one more for the road' – knowing that it will lead to a bad result but setting that aside emotionally so they can keep on boozing. A person can know what they should be doing, but feel it is OK for them not to do it.

Here's how to avoid regretting anything important:

1   If you blame something – or someone – else for your own lack of achievement, you are fooling no one but yourself. Taking responsibility for what you do and the results you get is the key to changing those things that are not working for you. Start with the reality of your results and analyse them; take on board those things you like about the results you have achieved and notice what you did to secure them, then identify all those things you do not like and identify what you have done to secure those too. If you allow yourself to slip into 'blaming', the exercise will fail, and it will not help you, so man up and focus.

2   Pretending that you have goals and objectives but not really meaning them is a meaningless activity; it affects only you, the people you care about and your future. Be clear about what you really want, and not what you think you *ought* to want. There is a huge difference between your own authentic aspirations and those you feel you must achieve to prove to other people that you are OK. Be OK with your own goals and your own ambitions.

3   Recognise that possibility exists everywhere, and that success is not a linear path. It is not possible to pick a future, and draw a line between where you are now and where you would like to be, hoping that you can follow the line like some kind of pathway to success. Everyone travels on a winding road; it may sometimes loop back on itself and appear to be taking you further away from where you need to be, but knowing that you are doing what's necessary to move you eventually towards your goal will be enough to keep you on the right path.

How to avoid leaving your best behind

WTF just happened to performing at my best?

Victoria could have been terrific; instead she was terrified. That's why she blew her opportunity. She had one opportunity to stand up, speak up, and say what she needed to say, but when her big opportunity came, she wasn't up to it. It was both sad and unnecessary, because she had the skills to do what she needed to do. She just didn't do it. She thought of her 'big opportunity' as a big thing – and it wasn't. Big things are always made up of smaller pieces, and the smaller pieces are often easier to 'crack' than the big thing.

During her speech, Victoria's brain wouldn't function, her mouth felt full of cotton wool, and the words that spilled out made no sense. The attention she had paid to her appearance, the designer suit and Jimmy Choos did nothing to help her confidence when she needed them to.

If Victoria had remembered a lesson she had learned elsewhere, she could have been successful and 'performed' at this presentation as if she'd been the headline act in a top-class cabaret. You see, Victoria had always wanted to sing, but hadn't been confident enough to try. Eventually her husband persuaded her to start singing lessons with Anton.

Anton's music room contained a state-of-the-art studio with sound-deadening panels, and an open singing booth complete with video camera. His students went away with a quality recording of their own voice after their lesson, and a video of what they looked like when singing. Anton believed that what you hear in your head and what other people might hear are two very different things, and that what you are really doing with your face and body as you sing will almost always surprise you.

This is true for almost all communication: what you do matters as much as what you intend to do, or what you think you are doing. Anton's mantra was: once you know what you must do, then all you need to do is to focus on doing it. It doesn't matter if one person or ten thousand people are listening; what you must do, and therefore how you sound, will be the same.

Victoria went to singing lessons and did well; no one was as surprised as she was when Anton asked her to join his choir, and at her first concert she performed solo for part of a song. Her confidence in her singing went through the roof. Unfortunately, she didn't transfer that new-found confidence into another, very important, part of her life: a place where personal confidence is necessary and valued – work. Victoria's job involved managing relationships between managers, donors, supporters, academics and volunteers. She had been with her company for just under a year and already there was pressure for instigating performance changes in those parts of the organisation represented by her team. This wasn't personal, and she didn't think it was, but it did put her in the position of conflicting with her peers, all of whom were nervous about how they might be affected by any changes. The board would be the final decision-makers. No final decision would be taken until after the next board meeting, before which each head of department was to be invited to present their case before the board, the trustees and a cross-section of interested parties. This would be Victoria's first opportunity to speak in front of such a large and influential audience since joining the company. It was actually her first opportunity ever to speak to such a large audience – of over two hundred people – in this, or any other, job.

When they were told about it, her colleagues who would also be speaking seemed to take it in their stride. However, Victoria was horrified, and terrified. Her team depended on her to speak up and make their case. She fervently believed in her position, and knew deep inside that the course she was advocating was the best course for the organisation, for her team and for herself. She was also absolutely convinced that her peers who were opposing her point of view were doing so out of self-interest, and that they did not have anyone's best interests at heart – except their own. It was therefore vital that she made a good job of it: she had to get her point across and she had to convince them that she was right.

Victoria took this very seriously. She wrote out her speech, read and reread it, made alterations again and again, and even recorded herself on her iPhone reading it. She knew there was no substitute for practice, and she could only have one chance. As the speech grew nearer, she found herself struggling to think of anything else. Her husband had been helpful and suggested it would be better if she sounded like she knew what she was saying rather than reading a prepared statement. It was good advice with which she agreed, so every night after dinner he helped her go over it again and again, until finally she knew her speech well enough to sound like she was saying it without reading it. On the day, she was ready. Or was she?

She wasn't first up, but watching some of her peers looking unprofessional and hapless up there on the big stage only served to bolster her confidence. She really was ready. Then she was given the cue by the conference host, and walked onto the stage. This is when it happened. Her mouth went dry, she started to sweat, her tummy began doing cartwheels, and all she could hear above the pounding in her head were her own words: 'I can't do this! I can't do this! I can't do this!' over and over. She stood there in abject panic. Her presentation was a stuttering and squeaky facsimile of the fantastic renditions she had achieved in front of her husband in their living room. She didn't even convince herself with her speech, never mind the audience, and so she wasn't surprised when later that evening the board decided in favour of one of her peers. A few days later, she received formal notice of redundancy. It shouldn't have happened. She thought she was ready, but if she really had been ready she wouldn't have screwed up so badly. She was outwardly prepared but hadn't considered the emotion of the moment. As Anton was always telling the choir: it is no good singing like a rock star in your bedroom but then being overtaken by nerves when the spotlight appears and the audience are waiting with anticipation. He told them over and over again that learning the words is not enough, because to perform you must speak from the heart and believe what comes out of your mouth – and be consistent whether the auditorium is empty or full. Victoria hadn't accounted for her emotions, and that lack of emotional preparation cost her dearly.

> There's just you, and what you do.

Her WTF moment came not long after she cleared her desk. It happened when she was on the way to Anton's for a lesson. She realised that the rules for a singing performance were no different from performing a speech. She realised that she'd known what to do all along, but hadn't done it. She had compartmentalised a singing performance in one box, and doing the work presentation in another – but putting them in boxes had been her mistake. She realised that there are no boxes unless you create them. There's just you, and what you do. She realised Anton was right: there was no difference between what she had done in her living room and what she should have done on the stage. If she had focused on what she was doing rather than what the audience might be thinking, things would have unfolded differently. The fact remains that there is no second chance. You only get one chance. Blow it, and it's gone.

Coaching psychologists make their living from people who know what they can do, but who didn't do it when it counted - just like Victoria. Career advisors spend a good deal of their time unpicking the core skills from a person's work history so that they can identify them, build on them, and use them to 'sell' the person into a new job, which might well be in a very different sphere. People are not very good at making these kinds of distinction because of something called chunking. They chunk one activity with another and then wrap them up in a context. A bartender may only see themselves working behind a bar because they've chunked all the individual elements of their job under the title of bartender. But skill in handling cash, dealing with queuing customers, building client relationships, courteously dealing with people who lose emotional control, and using a computerised system may be just the skills required in, for instance, a bank or an airport.

It's a little like a bowl of mayonnaise, it's now perceived as the whole and not its parts. Mayonnaise is made from eggs, oil, vinegar and mustard. It may not be possible to use the ingredients for something else once they're mixed together, but before they are mixed, they have all kinds of other uses. People are just like the ingredients for mayonnaise: they're more flexible and have more potential than they imagine.

Here's how to avoid being as inflexible as a salad dressing:

1 Become conscious of what you do, and how you do it. The end result comes about because of a combination of behaviours that you must do. You don't own the result; you own the ingredients that make up the result, but it's always up to you to put them together.

2 Don't be thrown by changes in circumstances. It's funny when you hear a child say, 'Don't watch me, I can't do it when you watch,' but it's not at all amusing for an adult to act the same way. Do what you need to do, wherever you need to do it.

3 Create your own alter ego. Superman needed Clark Kent and Batman, Bruce Wayne, but Superman was always Superman beneath those horn-rimmed glasses, and Bruce Wayne was still himself behind the black mask. In real life as well as in comic fantasies, people may find it helpful to create an alternative version of themselves that they know will perform better in certain situations.

Some people go into business. Some spend their career working for someone else. Whatever route a person takes, they all have decisions to make along the way, and in order to make those decisions they will always engage in discussion. Some people have those discussions with other people, but some don't bother going outside their own head. I don't mean that they don't talk to anyone about what they're going to do, but that there are some people who have already made their decisions after a conversation with themselves. Guess what? It's not always clever to trust your conscious thinking to help you make the best decisions about your future. It's not clever because your unconscious knows lots of stuff that could be helpful, but unless you engage with someone else to help prompt you to ask better questions and think differently, then these facts will remain undiscovered, and your decisions will be the worse for it. That's what happened to Carolyn and started her journey towards rock bottom.

Carolyn ended up on the street when she thought she was heading for a mansion. She made decisions about her future without speaking to, or listening to, anyone. She was wrong a good deal of the time, but she wouldn't admit it when she'd made a mistake. However, owning up to getting something wrong is good for us – it's a strength. It's why those people who do admit when they're wrong, and learn from their mistakes, stand a better chance of being successful. Unfortunately, Carolyn thought being wrong was a weakness. Shame, really, because if that had been different, she could have made something of herself. But when people like Carolyn make it clear how they feel about needing to be right all the time, other people tend to let them get away with it. They can't be bothered to get into an argument, and so take the easy road. Which is why whenever Carolyn came up with another of her hare-brained schemes, instead of asking her better questions that could have prevented her from failing, everybody told her it was a fabulous idea. Of course, they weren't the ones putting their homes on the line to get the idea off the ground.

Carolyn wasn't stupid, poorly educated or badly trained. She hadn't wasted her time working as the regional manager for a huge UK retailer; she knew all about producing targets and meeting the needs of the market, and she was good at being an operations manager. She knew what to look for and, better still, she knew how high to jump when things started to go wrong. So the idea of hitting 'stretching' targets didn't frighten her. Nor did the gloom-mongering of her friends who were brave enough to say so and put up with Carolyn ignoring whatever input they tried to offer her. However, Carolyn's WTF moment happened one sleepless night, when it finally dawned on her that her new business venture wasn't going to meet its payroll that week. There was no money left to tide it over, and no way that her bank would bail her out. Quite the opposite; she was in deep trouble. She knew that was true as soon as her banker got wind of the extent of the mess she was in. She knew the bank would want to try to claw back their relatively small investment, and wouldn't give a flying fig about Carolyn's life.

In her rush to get her idea off the ground she'd borrowed money and signed papers that meant she had to move from her family home. This wasn't a mortgaged bungalow with a little bit of equity; it was the home owned by her father and his father before him. Her failure meant she would have to move out and camp out with any friends who were prepared to help until she could find enough cash to rent a flat. The thought of living out of a suitcase and moving from friend to friend until she could get a job and get back on her feet wasn't pleasant. When the moment hit, she felt physically sick. It may not have been the worst moment of her life, but it was close. If ever there was a moment to say WTF?, this was it.

The reason people often say that a person can be their own worst enemy is that it's true, they can. Not just when they have an obvious problem, like alcoholism, but also when they get an idea into their head that they just can't shake, one that they become more and more enthused with, and then they buy in to their own idea with complete conviction. They are their own worst enemy because they wouldn't behave that way if someone else tried to sell them the idea; they wouldn't do it if even a trusted friend or relative tried to convince them, but when it's their own brainchild they can lose all sense, common or otherwise. This is what happened to Carolyn. It all started, like most tragic stories, with a heated conversation with a friend after Carolyn had already had a conversation inside her own head and made up her mind. Her friend tried to help her, tried to ask her better questions, but she was having none of it.

'It's a no-brainer! I can't believe no one has done this before; there's such a huge market for it and all I need to do is be there to take advantage of it.'

'How sure are you, Carolyn?' was the response from her best friend, Jane.

Carolyn was immediately defensive. 'Come on, Jane, you know me well enough don't you? Look, I wouldn't even be talking about it if I didn't think it would work!'

Jane didn't want to throw cold water on her friend's idea but was clearly concerned that Carolyn was getting carried away by her own enthusiasm.

'OK, I understand, but what research have you done?'

Even more defensive now, Carolyn started to get really annoyed. 'Stop being so dull, Jane. I'm sure the research is out there, but you only have to look around. I don't need a research document to tell me what my eyes can see – it's bloody obvious.'

Undeterred, Jane wasn't going to let her friend try to save her from what looked like pure hubris. 'OK then, if it's so obvious, please tell me why hasn't anyone already done it?'

Clearly very close to getting angry, Carolyn snapped back, 'I've been in retail for long enough to know what I'm looking at. Niche markets are where it's at, and this niche is huge.'

Jane knew she wasn't making headway but tried one last time, 'I know you think you know what you're doing but what if you're wrong? Don't you think you're being a little rash?'

Carolyn's final words on the subject were, 'I'm not wrong. I know what I'm doing, and the one person I thought I could count on to be there for me was you.'

With that, Carolyn stormed out of the bar, and even though Jane made numerous attempts to contact her again, it was the last conversation they had. Perhaps if they had met again or at least talked shortly afterwards it would have been OK, but the longer the silence went on the more awkward it felt.

Carolyn wouldn't listen to anyone who had a bad word to say about her business concept. In her mind, there was no room for criticism, and she thought that the more fervently she believed in its success, the more likely that success would be. She was wrong – dreadfully wrong. The business failed, she failed and her life failed. Tragically, if she had only listened, if she had just let go of her own certainty, it could all have been avoided. She was arrogant and wouldn't listen to anyone, however. The longer this went on, the more isolated she became, which meant when something didn't pan out as she'd been so sure it would, she was left alone. She had nowhere to go, no one to turn to and nothing to fall back on. She had bought into her own idea, hook, line and sinker, and it had well and truly sunk her.

I won't dwell on Carolyn's fall from grace, apart from to say that she couldn't find a job of the kind she wanted without having a permanent address, and by the time she lowered her sights her standards had dropped too. She could only get through the day with a drink, then another drink ... Now a self-confirmed alcoholic, she has still to hit rock bottom, and although friends have reached out to her, suggested Alcoholics

Anonymous, offered to pay for therapy or support her through rehab, she's having none of it. As far as she's concerned, the problem is not as big as everyone else makes it out to be, and she believes she's lost everything anyway and so has nothing else to lose. She's learned nothing; she's still making life decisions after only discussing them with herself.

Psychological research tells us that not only do people believe their own lies even when they acknowledge to themselves that they are indeed lying, but also that they will only change their destructive behaviour once it is less painful to do so than not change. Alcoholics are known to have to hit rock bottom before they will ask for help and genuinely mean it, and smokers can ignore all manner of health warnings, but the moment their darling child looks them in the eye and, with a tear falling down a rosy cheek, pleads, 'Please don't smoke and die, Daddy,' then the pain of quitting might, on balance, become the better choice. A balance of pain and pleasure may exist in the realm of human decision-making, but the factor that really makes a difference is the balance between 'pain' and 'more pain'. Everything a person does carries some level of pain: if you want them to change their behaviour then you must make changing less painful than continuing with what they're doing. However, the pain can never be done to them; it must be something they do to themselves. If you attempt to inflict pain to force a person to change, they will find a way of subverting you, but if you can encourage them to find their own pain, they will seek a way to make it go away.

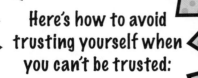

Here's how to avoid trusting yourself when you can't be trusted:

1 Start with the premise that you might be wrong rather than the certainty that you are right. Don't lower your levels of confidence or certainty in your own ability, but recognise that you are fallible, you are human, and humans make mistakes.

2 Good ideas are ten a penny, but great ideas are rare. Good ideas often don't stand up to closer scrutiny and the harsh spotlight of objective feedback, whereas great ideas stand up to the closest investigation and the most determined criticism. Therefore, invite criticism and encourage research and investigation, because it is better to know in advance that something may not work as well as you hope it will than find out after you have invested your time ~ and cash ~ into the idea.

3 Hang on to your friends even when they don't agree with you. Friendship and support will matter most to you when things go wrong. It's not difficult to find people to celebrate with you when you are successful, but it's tough to find real friends when your world falls apart. Good friends are a way of protecting yourself from yourself, so that if things get really bad and go terribly wrong you have people who care enough about you to stick with you, even when you're at your worst.

Akiko was just doing what she thought was right - like a footballer shooting at goal when passing to another player may have been the better decision. A goal may not be guaranteed, but I guarantee you this: the passionate fans in the crowd couldn't care less who scores the goal; all they care about is that *someone* scores. In that moment, the football crowd is the epitome of being outcome-driven. Success is uppermost in their mind. There are other times when the crowd is the opposite of that, and becomes ego-focused instead - when things aren't going their team's way and people want to vent their emotion, when people blame a player or the manager unfairly, or call for change just for change's sake.

The difference between being outcome-driven and ego-focused is the difference between sustainable success and abject failure. Hence, doing what you think is right when it's actually ego-focused will always be a mistake.

Akiko's story will resonate with anyone who might have felt misunderstood, and it brings into sharp relief the tough choices that have to be made when your future is at stake.

Akiko moved continents to further her career, but then she quit her job and walked away from a promising career. The outcome she wanted was a glittering future, but that's not what she got. She blames her ex-boss, her ex-boss's boss and the company. The truth is that there was a problem. However, perhaps it was a problem that could, and should, have been dealt with. The reality was that the company loved Akiko, and they didn't want her to quit, but she didn't think she had any choice. The fallout ruined not only her career, but damaged her boss's immediate career prospects too. He had also adopted an ego-focused attitude, and it didn't do him any good either.

Geoff, her boss, was no management angel, but he was no devil in disguise either. He'd been with the company for about a year, so had already moved past the early days of having to prove himself. Geoff was on his best behaviour in this job: moving there had been a big step up in his career, and he'd been ultra-keen to be the best manager he could be. Geoff recognised that perhaps he'd been a bit of a hothead in the past. Previous feedback confirmed that sometimes he opened his mouth before putting his brain in gear, so he had tried hard to stop himself making similar mistakes in his new role. He thought he'd done well, but had also recognised that he was at risk of his emotions sometimes getting the better of him. So he'd done his best to build a relationship with each of his direct reports that was strong enough to over-come any faux pas he might make, and in his mind had made a special effort with Akiko, which is why he felt so aggrieved when it all went pear-shaped.

Some WTF moments are born out of outrage and bewilderment. This was the case for Akiko. Her moment happened when Geoff told her she was being 'stubborn and pig-headed'. Although she had been living in the UK for more than two decades, and had got used to many of the differences in culture, this was a step too far for her. Back home in the small Hong Kong company she worked for, she had in many ways expected far worse behaviour from her bosses, but this was different. Joining a big international organisation and moving to another country had raised her expectations. She had become good at recognising when a boss had his own prejudices: about women (and about young women in particular) and about expectations of employees. When she could link what she considered was their issue, not hers, to their behaviour, then she could let it go. When she couldn't, and when she had to accept that this was a direct and very blunt criticism of her, then it felt very different. This was her ego rearing its ugly head. The reason why people use the saying 'get off your high horse' is that falling from the beast flipping well hurts. So, if you are going to take offence about something, stop and think for a second before climbing up onto that stallion. It may be better for you to just suck it up and move on. Sometimes it's better to be successful than to be right. Akiko had her view, her boss didn't see things the same way, and his boss had his own take on things. So, which view is true, which is the 'truth', and what really matters?

Three people (the boss, the boss's boss and an apparently neutral third party from the HR department): three perspectives, and three very different experiences. Yet, when all is said and done, Akiko only had one outcome that really mattered to her, but she let her ego get in the way.

Geoff's point of view: 'I'm not stupid, but I also know I've got a lot to learn. I'm thirty-five and already further ahead in my career than I thought I would be when I left university, so I was pleased about that until this happened. Akiko leaving in the way she did is devastating because I know she blames me for it, I know that the company blame me for it, and to be honest, I now blame myself as well. I don't blame myself for her going, just for getting into trouble because of it. I'm glad she's gone: she was always moaning and complaining, so we are better off without her. If I knew then what I know now, then things would be different, but they're not. Off the record, I'm also frustrated and angry with her: why didn't she tell me how she was feeling? Why didn't she say something until it was too late? Why couldn't she speak to me? I thought I'd done everything I could to make her feel at ease with me, so what's her problem? Not only has she screwed her own career, she's also thrown a grenade into mine, and that doesn't feel fair. Whatever her problem is, she's made it my problem now as well, which is frustrating because I know I should have just put her through a formal disciplinary procedure instead of trying to chat to her. I should have made it HR's problem, not mine. As it is, this will hang over me for years. I might as well start looking for another job now because I doubt I'll be going anywhere with this company now she's put her oar in. You know what they say: throw enough mud and some of it will stick. Well, she threw more than enough in my direction. They've now put me on another training course which is just repeating what I already know, and given me a mentor. This is wasting my time as well as costing the company a small fortune; I'm not learning anything new, and my mentor is the same age as me, doing the same type of job as me, and no more qualified to tell me what to do than I am. The company's just covering its backside and blaming me, when what they really should be saying is "good riddance to bad rubbish".'

Geoff's boss's point of view might as well be about a different situation completely. Did he even know what was going on? He said: 'Akiko was a great asset to this company. We value and respect people in this organisation, and strive to value our differences rather than see them as a source of conflict. Geoff was unable to effectively manage Akiko and support her when she was dealing with a tough supplier issue. Having reviewed the case, I have no doubt that Akiko was working in our best interest. My view is that she required appropriate support from her line manager, rather than personal attacks on her ability to perform in her job. I regret that she has left us, and can only hope that the remedial support we are now providing for Geoff ensures that in the future he meets the required standards of leadership we demand from our managers.'

The third-party observer's point of view might be unkindly perceived by some as less of a point of view and more a 'CYA' (Cover Your Ass-ets) statement: 'Akiko was on a career path with us that, as a next step, would have seen her managing her own department. She didn't know that her name was already attached to a new opening and that within weeks she could have been taking up the new post. The unfortunate situation with her manager was unnecessary. Since being given responsibility for a particular project, Akiko had been working on a supplier problem, a problem that had been recognised and ignored because it was very challenging. Unlike others, she hadn't caved in and taken the easy route of allowing things to stand, but had insisted that the supplier adapt to the company's terms and conditions if it wanted to continue doing business with us. The supplier was known to rely on an informal relationship with someone very senior in our business, and had threatened to cause problems if she persisted. Akiko persisted, which in turn caused the supplier to speak to their senior advocate, who in turn put pressure on Geoff. Unfortunately, Geoff did not support Akiko, but appears to have attempted to curry favour by "having a word with her", as it had been intimated he do. His approach to "having a word with her" was to publicly admonish her in front of the rest of the team, and to call her "stubborn and pig-headed". In actual fact, these are attributes he might have been better acknowledging as a strength, and he should have supported Akiko in using her natural tenacity to achieve a better result for the company. The senior individual concerned has now made it very clear that, had he known the truth about the problems reported to him by his supplier contact, he would have supported Akiko himself. As might be expected with the issue coming to light, it was this senior individual who requested the agreement with the supplier be terminated and a new supplier sought, which is what Akiko had been arguing for, had been seeking support from Geoff for, and which was the issue about which she had been "stubborn and pig-headed". It is such a shame she left us. We did all we could to convince her to stay, but she could not see past the issue, and I suppose that same stubbornness might have been stopping her from letting it go.'

These three points of view are from three people looking at the same set of events through ego-focused glasses: a manager making excuses for handling a situation badly, a more senior manager attempting to sound so politically correct that he can't be held to account, and an organisation's representative determined to 'present their case'. Here's the point: Akiko could not control anyone's actions but her own. If she had forgotten about her ego and focused instead on the outcome, there is every chance she would have achieved a better result.

She is one of those people whose potential hasn't been realised, not because she didn't have the opportunity, but because she allowed something to get in the way. Her priority needed to be herself, not her wounded pride, slighted feelings, or whatever else was getting in the way of her outcome. She needed to be like that football crowd cheering for their team and hoping beyond hope that they would score a goal, however the ball ended up in the back of the net.

Akiko's not the first person to have a boss who may not (in their employees' eyes) deserve their job: a boss who is immature, a boss who thinks they are better than they are, a boss who believes everyone else is stupid, a boss who says one thing and does another. Nor will she be the last. However, just because a boss is one – or even all – of those things doesn't mean that their subordinates can't achieve their potential.

> All she had to do was step up and focus on her outcome, and she could have walked through an open door to new opportunities.

I don't know what Akiko was hoping for, but my guess is probably nothing. I think Akiko was just stuck in the situation and couldn't see it objectively. If she could have stepped up and had a go at seeing things from Geoff's point of view, she would have realised what an ass she was being. If she had stepped up to see herself through the eyes of Geoff's boss, perhaps she would have been enlightened, and if she'd stepped up to take a peek at the situation through the detached view of the HR manager she would have seen things as they are and not as they felt. All she had to do was step up and focus on her outcome, and she could have walked through an open door to new opportunities.

Psychology has long proposed that there is always a balance between how events are interpreted for what they are and how they affect a person. Known as 'Cognitive Evaluation Theory', the concept is simply that things that happen to us are interpreted by the person experiencing them. This means that two people can experience a very similar event and yet respond to it in very different ways. To one person the event means one thing and to another, something else entirely. The interpretations are different because people are different; we all observe our reality and unconsciously ask ourselves, 'Can I handle this, or not?' We also can't help thinking about the cause of whatever we are experiencing; if it feels like our own fault (even if it's not) then it has an effect on our internal motivation, but if we unconsciously accept that we bear no responsibility for the cause of those events (even if we are in some part to blame) then it doesn't affect our motivation anywhere near as much. A shorthand version of this that is easier to comprehend and to apply is the difference between being ego-focused or outcome-driven. The choice of which to be is a conscious one and therefore can be made by all of us. Making a decision can increase the level of confidence we feel in handling a situation, and also the extent to which we blame ourselves for events. Broadly speaking, an ego-focused approach will be less empowering and cause a person to feel more responsible for the event – not a good thing. Whereas an outcome-driven approach is more likely to increase confidence in finding a way of dealing with events, and it is also more likely to emotionally distance a person from blame for the cause of events – a good thing.

Here's how to step up when you need to:

1   There's a rule: the more the boss has to prove a case, the less likely it is that the case can be proved. People in positions of power are just people: they are as fallible as anyone else, and sometimes, when you can't believe they've been given their job, they can't believe it either. So there's no need to treat them as if they are the police or that you're in the forces and they can put you on the front line whether you like it or not (unless of course you are in the forces). Their job is to support you to do a better job. Part of that support may be to stop you failing, so you may need them to steer you on occasion, but they are not there for any other reason than to 'be there' for you.

2   You don't know everything, so don't pretend that you do. If you don't ask better questions, then you won't get better answers. You only ever get to see your view of everything, so you must step out of your own certainty and step up into accepting someone else's. They may not be any more 'right' than you are, but they have their own point of view and they have as much right to it as you do to yours. It requires some stepping up to be able to let go of your own certainty and accept someone else's, even for a short while, but the benefits of stepping up are that you get to ask much better questions; questions like, 'If I were in their shoes how might I see things differently?' 'When have I been surprised to be wrong in the past?' or even 'How can I use the situation to my advantage even though I wouldn't necessarily choose to be here?' Ask better questions of yourself and you will find that the answers you get are inevitably more helpful.

3   If you had a crystal ball that showed you you'd be successful, then you would be much more likely to step up. A little like if you knew in advance what the lottery numbers were going to be, then you might just buy a ticket. Billions of people all over the world play anyway, even though they don't know what the numbers are, in the hope that they might be lucky. Often the cost of a lottery ticket is worth the weekly hope that comes with it: maybe this week it'll be my numbers? Maybe it's my time? Some people argue that playing the lottery is a waste of money; they argue that each time they *don't* buy a ticket, the money they would have spent goes to buying something they know they want and know they will be able to afford one day. Their certainty about their future is a bigger emotional attraction than the lottery player's eternal hope. What they have in common is a dream for the future: they aren't caught up in today's problems, but are dreaming about the benefits a new tomorrow could bring.

How to avoid being steamrollered by circumstance

WTF just happened to making the most of my life?

Johnny made some bad choices, but being who he is isn't one of them. Johnny's problems don't stem from any issue with his identity, but with the way he handled confusion, and the way he allowed external circumstances to drive his internal judgements. With hindsight, he realised that it should have been the other way around. Of course, that's easy to say. I'd be amazed if you could tell me, hand on heart, you have never made a poor judgement call in your life, and if you did I'm afraid I probably wouldn't believe you. That's because I've never met anyone who doesn't regret *something*. It's not what we do that makes us successful; it's what we do about what we've done wrong that shapes the person we become and that influences the people we have in our lives. However, I accept that Johnny's little mistake was maybe not so little, and needed a whole lot of reflecting to put it right.

Sometimes you think you have no choice but you actually have the most powerful choice of all, and it's not possible to be steamrollered into making bad decisions when you realise how much choice you really have. Everyone has some level of will to be the best they can be, and make the most of their life, but to access this will and use it means recognising that circumstances are not the sole determinant of your future, that you are in charge of your own future.

Having attended lots of motivational talks over the years, I've heard various versions of the American airman story (briefly, he was imprisoned, with little or no opportunity for exercise, yet came out of prison playing better golf than he had when he went in).* Methinks the late Mr Ziglar, Mr Dyer, and the still very much alive Mr Robbins may have taken a few liberties with the truth, but no matter, because the idea is sound: being shut up in a prison cell only imprisons the body, not the mind. They may have been referring to a certain Colonel George Hall who, after more than seven years' imprisonment, and having shed about 100 lb, apparently played to his handicap the first time he played golf afterwards. When accused of beginner's luck, he argued that he hadn't 'three-putted a green in the past seven years', as he'd played golf over and over in his mind.

Colonel Hall is no average man, because the average person kept in those conditions for that long did not come out playing golf as if it were only last weekend they'd swung a club. Most came out mentally wrecked. Now, it would be deeply unkind to call them losers, but in contrast to Colonel Hall they can't be considered anything else. Of course they weren't to blame – they were victims, but that's the point. Being a victim of your own circumstance is a choice, not an inevitability. Did Colonel Hall want to be in prison? No! Did he like being there? No! Did he give in to those circumstances and give up on himself? No! But most people do. Most people accept 'average' as their lot, and ignore the possibility of reaching our potential to be 'normal'.

Before going any further, let me explain what I mean by 'normal' in this instance because I'm not simply using it as a synonym for average. I'm referring to the concept of something called 'normalcy', meaning fit for purpose. A washing machine working normally washes clothes and does what is expected of it. An average washing machine may not clean clothes as well as some, but better than others.

....

* See http://www.consistentgolf.com/mind-control-for-golf-improvement/.

In this context, being normal means living up to your own potential as opposed to being average. Average might mean you are a better performer than some, and not as good as others, but you still don't achieve your own potential. The goal for all of us has to be to achieve our own standard of normalcy or personal normality – to function in the best way we can, and not judge ourselves harshly or settle for being 'average'.

Johnny's WTF moment happened when it dawned on him he might have made a mistake that would be hard to recover from. Johnny grew up in East Ham, London, a timid boy, more interested in West Side Story than West Ham. All the other boys labelled him as 'gay', and while at first this was a taunt, it wasn't long before he was just accepted the way he was, and none of his mates cared who he was attracted to. After all, it was the 1990s and they had grown up with Frankie Goes To Hollywood, the Communards and Boy George. It wasn't a crime, nor was being different a reason to be ridiculed; on the whole, and for most of his peers, boys like Johnny were accepted for who they were, or more accurately 'who other people assumed they were', and differences between each other were celebrated.

However, some of his schoolmates couldn't help themselves when it came to 'banter'. That's what they called it, but really it was hateful prejudice aimed at making themselves feel superior, and was just nasty. Johnny had put up with 'banter' from those kids throughout his formative years. He had worked hard at his physique so that at least they'd respect his ability to flex muscles that most of them could only dream of. He'd developed a six-pack while they'd been working on growing beer bellies.

Johnny was conflicted. He had tried forming relationships with other boys, but his heart just wasn't in it. He'd had sex many times, but only after getting high or downing a tray full of shots. Then, not quite out of the blue but still as a surprise, it hit him that he couldn't conform to the label (of being gay) he'd applied to himself. Not only did he quite fancy women, but there was one in particular he'd seen, and was strongly attracted to. He'd never felt like this before. He couldn't stop thinking about Joanne. He had to meet her, but how could he do that when everyone knew he was gay – and didn't know that really he wasn't?

Finally, Johnny came up with a plan. He would make up a new past, walk away from everyone and everything he knew, and start again as a straight guy with an amazing physique, and go out with the raven-haired beauty he couldn't stop dreaming about. It was a plan — not a good plan, but at least he'd given it a bit of thought. What he failed to consider was that, while he might leave the past behind, the past might not so easily let go of him. In his race to escape, he imagined that he was caught in the trap of his past and believed he had no choice but to play the hand he was dealt. He was only partly correct, because there isn't just one way of playing it.

> The trouble was, the more he got into the deception, the more he realised what a terrible plan it had been.

When he met Joanne, he worked hard to hide any trace of his past life. They met at restaurants he scoped out, but had never been to before, and he opened a new Facebook account using his first and middle names. He filled it with photos of himself or places he had been, and left it at that. She never knew his real surname, so there was no chance of her Googling him, and he told her he'd been working abroad, so there was no way for her to track him down via work either. The trouble was, the more he got into the deception, the more he realised what a terrible plan it had been. Within weeks she was asking questions about his family and friends, and was clearly surprised by his reticence to share information. After six months of him regularly changing the password on his phone so she couldn't read his text messages, and never meeting any of his friends or family, she knew something wasn't right. When her family met him, they were less forgiving than she was: they speculated that he might have come out of prison, been in a gang, or even be on a witness protection programme. Clearly, they watch too much TV. The thing was, all this intrigue was unspoken but clearly felt: you could cut the tension with a knife, and it was forcing her into being ever more protective of him.

That was, until the day she stopped being protective, the day she'd had enough of the intrigue, the day Johnny's tight-lipped refusal to share anything of himself broke their relationship. By then, as unlikely as it sounds, they had moved in together. He convinced her to pool her resources and they'd bought a house in joint names. I don't think Johnny could quite believe it himself, but he'd managed to manipulate her into almost accepting him without a past. Almost, but not quite. The bit he didn't manage was to believe in it himself. He was still surviving by living a lie. He was still responding as a victim of his circumstances, and therefore could never love her in the way she needed to be loved and reassured. He couldn't reassure himself, so he had no chance of doing it for her. Yet, despite the odds, he had nearly made it. On average he'd done well, but he wasn't living up to his potential – so 'average' leads to being a loser.

Johnny had to be 'normal' for him to win. To use an analogy, don't think of a person for a moment, but think of a car. When you buy a new car, do you want it to work normally, or do you want to look at all the breakdowns that could occur and be happy that your car performs averagely well? I hope you want to buy one that works as it should, that works 'normally'. When it breaks down, that's abnormal. Therefore, people who behave normally do so to their full potential; they 'work' as well as they are able, and while normality is different for different people, it is always better than average.

Johnny was being 'average', Colonel Hall was being 'normal': an average person would not have responded in the way that he did. A person without his resolve might not have had the ability to respond in the way that he did, but for the Colonel this was his normal. Johnny lost Joanne because he allowed the situation to overwhelm him, yet he most probably had the potential within him to rise above it. He didn't and he lost. Losing happens when you accept your circumstances and pretend that you have no choice but to give in. That is never true; you always have the choice to be normal, to be the best you can be in those circumstances, and to focus on where you eventually want to be rather than where you are now.

Would Joanne have accepted Johnny if he'd come clean and told her the truth? We will never know. All we can know is that at least he would have increased the odds of hanging on to her. He had once been confused about his sexuality. Trying to hide this period of his life created the problem. As it was, choosing to respond as if he had no choice was always going to lead to the inevitable. It's a shame, because it need not have been that way. Making a mistake doesn't prevent anyone from reaching their true potential. Johnny could have behaved in a way that matched his true purpose and capability.

> As it was, choosing to respond as if he had no choice was always going to lead to the inevitable.

Psychologists point out that our expectations often dictate our experiences. It's not so much 'you can if you believe you can' as 'if you believe you can't then you won't'. In the nicest possible way, nobody except Johnny cares very much about his sexual orientation. Thankfully, we live in a world where sexuality is merely one aspect of a person. However, if a person makes an issue out of any aspect of their 'being', it is likely to become a problem.

Here's how to avoid sabotaging yourself:

1 Recognise the things that are happening to you as opposed to the things you are making happen. Ignorance is not bliss, because at some point you will become aware of what you have done. The things that happened to you haven't caused you to do whatever you did; they simply provided a background onto which you could act out your own play. The choices you made were yours, and although you may have made them unthinkingly, at some point you must begin to think for yourself.

2 Be prepared to change your mind. If you were driving somewhere and realised you were heading the wrong way, not only would you be prepared to change direction, but you'd also be ready to retrace your steps until you found the point at which you went wrong. Driving your life is no different; you can either pretend that the road you are on will be OK as long as you look at it through a different window, or you can see it for what it is, and change.

3 Listen to your inner voice. We all have one, but it will be drowned out by life if you never give it a chance to be heard. Anyone who tells you there's no such thing as an inner voice is probably the kind of person who lives amid constant noise: they move from real conversations to being distracted by the radio; put the TV on as soon as they get home, without even really listening to it; and don't give themselves even a moment of quiet contemplation. Your inner voice could be screaming at you to see things in a different way, but if you don't give yourself the opportunity to hear it then you are likely to remain in ignorance, and may fail to live the life you really want.

Do you have a bucket list? You know, a list of things that you want to do before you die? If you do, how are you doing with it? If you died now, would you be happy that you'd ticked off enough of your list? If you don't have a list, is this because you imagine that there will be plenty of time for that kind of thing in the future, or because you think you'll never die, or is it something else? Whatever it is, there is only one thing that we can all be sure of … and it isn't that we will have time to complete a bucket list.

Jan was complacent: she had her future planned in detail, but never had the chance to carry those plans through. She is not alone. If I had a pound for every story I've been told like this one, I'd have a ton of cash. All I can say, before you get into this story, is this: your clock is ticking right now. Time won't wait for you to put your plans in motion, so flipping well get on with it.

Jan was a terrific pianist and played the violin like a virtuoso. She was so good that she was spotted early, and got a paying job as a session musician. It never amounted to much, though, with one small job giving way to another, and so on. Life was tough. She learned not to make plans because she didn't know where she'd be, what she'd do or who she'd be with in a week or a month, never mind a year. It was a hand-to-mouth life, and although she loved it, she hated its insecurity just as much. So when Don came into her life it was as if he was the missing piece of her life's puzzle. Not everything changed, but all the insecure bits of her life went away. He was financially stable and wanted to be there for her whenever she needed him.

He came to see her perform regularly – not often enough to be creepy or stalker-ish, but often enough to show her that it was more than the music or that particular show that he was interested in. He'd meet her afterwards and buy her a late supper, even when he had to get up early for work the next day. He would bring her a packed lunch into the theatre on those long days just prior to opening when the longest break they'd get was half an hour between calls, and he was there for her when one job ended and she became convinced it would be her last. It never was, of course; there was always another offer of work, even if it took a few weeks to appear. Now she had Don, money was less of a worry. He was the stability she needed, so you won't be surprised that it wasn't long before dating turned into 'seeing each other officially'. That soon turned into being 'in a relationship', and this eventually led to marriage, at the old parish church where Jan had been christened.

It was a lovely day: the weather stayed dry for the photos and the reception was a triumph, with short speeches and long conversations over a glass of wine and a delicious meal. Jan had insisted on an evening party so that all her musician mates could celebrate her special day, and they did, in style. There was no disco for Jan and Don – not with a room full of professional musicians. They jammed, they sang, they played all her favourite tunes, and eventually let Don and Jan escape for their honeymoon, and it was during their honeymoon that the couple began to make their plans. Sitting on the balcony, overlooking the ocean as the sun made its way towards the horizon, they talked and talked about what their future would hold. They talked about the children they would bring into the world, and how they would raise them to be the best they could be. They talked about the house they would one day build, with its sound-proofed music studio for her, and man cave for him. They talked about how one day they would retire to a place just like the one they were in now: a place where they could sit on a balcony in the warmth and watch the sun go down every day, and a place where they could grow old and be as much in love with each other as they were now. The more they talked about their plans, the more real they seemed, and they did this every year: they sat on a balcony watching the sun go down somewhere in the world, talking about 'one day when ...' and all the things they wanted to do together. However, there was always something else that got in the way. There was the contract Jan won to play with a live orchestra on a TV show that was aired all over the world, which was so popular that it ran season after season. The job was so good that she couldn't step away from it and make time for having babies, as much as she claimed that she wanted to. Don was a patient man but, being fifteen years her senior, didn't really want to be mistaken for their children's grandfather when the time came. Even so, every year when contract time came around, Jan signed up for another season, unable to shake the old feeling that there might not be another job after this one. Don dutifully supported her and went along with it, always believing that maybe next year would be the one when they started their family and began the new life they'd spent so long planning.

Finally, there was just one week to go before the final televised show. Don, as always, had his ticket ready and planned to be there in the audience to see this year's celebrity crowned as the winner, and would be there to take Jan to their favourite bistro instead of the after-show party that neither of them enjoyed. He had a feeling that this year would be different: a feeling deep in his gut that there wouldn't be another TV season for Jan, and that maybe this year their plans would start in earnest. He was both right and wrong. On her way to final rehearsals, Jan collapsed. She was rushed to hospital, and by the time Don got there she was in surgery. She'd had an aneurism. It could have had a multitude of causes: her orchestra friends said that she hadn't been herself recently and had been 'a bit stressed' – but what about, and why, was anyone's guess. Jan had never been able to quit the smoking habit she'd picked up as a teenager, and had smoked a lot, so maybe this had contributed. At forty-three, she knew her window of opportunity for ever having a child was closing rapidly, so this too may have had something to do with it. No one could be sure.

Jan was kept alive for two days after the operation, but then, after several tests, was declared brain-dead. She was only breathing because she was attached to a respirator. Don sat with her for one final conversation before saying goodbye. He told her that one day, somehow, somewhere, they would be together again, and this time they would not let anything get in the way of finding their own balcony from which to watch the sun go down; that they would raise a family to share the warmth with them; and that this time they would make it happen. He leaned over, kissed her forehead for the final time, and said goodbye. Sad, so sad. For goodness' sake, if something is important to you, then get on with doing it.

We all know we are going to die, but we do our best to pretend that it will never happen. The jury is out as to precisely why this happens: some psychologists will tell you that it's a defence mechanism to keep us from becoming depressed, while some will tell you that such delusions are not limited to death, but apply to anything that threatens our day-to-day ability to survive, and others will tell you that we are all just hardwired to both accept and ignore the fact that, one day, the Grim Reaper will tell us it's our turn. Religion may be to blame for many things that are not helpful, but when it comes to death, each religion has its own take on what happens after we die. From reincarnation to Judgement Day, they all have one thing in common: that something else is in charge of our destiny, so we might as well do the best we can while we are on Earth, to give us the best opportunities in whatever follows. This acts as a mental comfort blanket, and doesn't need to be true in order to be useful, as it's proved to be helpful in allowing people to live a fulfilling and useful life.

WTF Just Happened?

Here's how to avoid complacency:

1   Embrace the concept of JFDI — just flipping do it (or words to that effect). JFDI is meant to suggest diving in without a thought for the consequences: to stop procrastinating and simply get on with it. If you want something, then it's up to you to make it happen. Often that means taking lots of small steps rather than one giant leap, so even if you can't yet see how to make your dreams come true, that's no reason to stop you taking a step towards them. Even a tiny step is better than no step at all.

2   Believe in yourself enough to make your plans real. You get one shot at this life, to do with it what you please, and if you don't take that opportunity then shame on you. If you want something, then find a way to start making it happen, because if you don't make a start then you have zero chance of ever finishing.

3   Let go of perfection, because all it will do is hold you back. Nothing a human being does in life is perfect, so it follows that your plans won't be perfect either. Flaws are a necessary part of your journey: you don't just plan to go through the motions; you plan to achieve things along the way, such as good feelings, kindness, love, helping your children be the best they can be, actually getting round to having children at all, and all those other things you want to be able to look back on when the time comes and say 'At least I did that.' So give yourself a kick in the pants if necessary, and start turning your plans into something real. No one cares if they're not perfect, and no one but you really cares if you do them at all, so you have to make them happen for *you* not for anyone else.

How to avoid wishing you hadn't given up

WTF just happened to my commitment?

In Alan's own words, he's a loser. But no one, including him, needs to be. You've had to wait until the final story in this book to find out the formula that will help stop you becoming a loser. It is a simple formula that anyone can apply, it will work for everyone, and it is guaranteed to work in any circumstances anywhere in the world. It's the formula for being a winner – personal development guru Tony Robbins calls it the 'Ultimate Success Formula'* – and it has just five steps. It goes like this:

Step 1: Know specifically, and with absolute clarity, precisely what you want.

Step 2: Know with complete emotional commitment *why* you want it.

Step 3: Make a significant, powerful and measurable move towards your ultimate goal that stimulates movement in its direction.

Step 4: Recognise and understand precisely what results you are getting from your actions.

Step 5: Make a choice – either keep going in the same direction or change direction if the results aren't giving you what you want. Change as many times as necessary.

....

* See T. Robbins, *Awaken the Giant Within* (London: Simon & Schuster, 1991), pp. 38–44.

Commitment isn't about being bloody-minded, arrogant or in some way singularly focused on your own goal. Effective commitment is more about having an approach that is consistent, which is what the 'Ultimate Success Formula' is all about. A lack of commitment – not necessarily a lack of clarity about a goal, but a lack of certainty and consistency – turns a person into a loser.

This was Alan's problem. This is why Alan became a loser. Alan didn't hold himself in high esteem. Referring to himself as an idiot and a fool and yet still ploughing on with the behaviour that caused him to become that way is not a very bright thing to do. He didn't become bitter about his predicament, just disappointed – and that's a horrible way to feel. It reminds me of when a child longs for its parents to tell him off and be angry, because although being told off is painful while it's happening, you know you'll get over it. Instead, those parents would look sad and tell the child how disappointed they were in him.

Is it likely that, later on in life, that person will still, at some level, be concerned about not disappointing their parents? Some people, even in adulthood, have a bigger than expected emotional response when they realise they were hoping for approval from Mum or Dad. It's unlikely that's what the parents intended but it's hardly helpful in building self-esteem and confidence. Even worse than that is disappointing yourself, which can dramatically undermine your self-esteem and confidence. Alan trusted his judgement when he had no right to trust it. He had nothing to base that trust on. He was a senior teacher in a sought-after school, so he held a position of trust, and in that role his judgement was rarely brought into question. However, outside school, he was as clueless as a first year at the start of term.

Alan was not only clueless; he was clueless about his cluelessness. Anne, his first wife, left him. She didn't leave because they grew apart, one of them had an affair or the numerous other common reasons for dumping a spouse. She left because when Alan made up his mind about something, *nothing* would get him to change it. After ten years of trying unsuccessfully for a child, Anne was desperate to give anything a go if it might lead to having a baby. She read somewhere that eating avocado every day was a good idea, so everything they ate was accompanied by an avocado salad; she understood exercise was an important issue, so she did classes at the gym and kept herself trim. She took on board everything that could help, but Alan had decided that, despite doctors' assurances to the contrary, there was something 'wrong' with Anne. He knew he wasn't shooting blanks, as he'd got a previous girlfriend pregnant. So, when Anne had finally had enough of his unspoken criticism and had run out of things to fix the problem, she left him.

As fate would have it, within a year Anne met someone else: a man with less 'certainty' than Alan and who didn't put her under the same stress Alan had done. Within six months, Anne was pregnant. Apparently, the only thing 'wrong' with her had been Alan. The fact that he had given up on her, and blamed her, had caused such stress that it had prevented her getting pregnant. There's little doubt that if Alan had been more relaxed, less convinced of his own 'rightness', and more willing to let his marriage play out by loving and supporting his wife, it might have been him bouncing bonny children on his lap rather than his replacement. His lack of commitment to the success of the marriage hadn't just failed the marriage; it had failed him too. If he'd known the formula and followed it, he would have had to behave differently.

Marriage wasn't Alan's only failure: like thousands of other people, he had bought his first house in the mid-1980s at inflated prices and had taken out an eye-watering mortgage just before the UK housing crash of '89. Unlike most people, who sat on their negative equity and rode it out until the market eventually caught up with what they'd paid, Alan was convinced that the market would never recover. He sold his house and took a huge loss that put him in debt for more than a decade. Convinced the market would never recover, he refused to buy again, and to this day still rents his modest home (at an ever-increasing rent). His salary hasn't kept up with rent increases, so every year sees him poorer than the last. While his peers have house-hopped up the housing ladder and acquired significant equity along the way, Alan hasn't. Alan's misplaced certainty in the death of the housing market wasn't his finest hour. His lack of commitment to his original decision to buy a house had not served him well. Again, the formula for success would have caused him to ask better questions and recognise when things were not going in the 'right' direction.

There's no doubt that Alan regrets his lack of commitment to Anne and his about-turn on the house-buying front, but the worst 'could have been' that haunts him is his point-blank refusal to embrace technology. Being a maths and physics teacher with a natural affinity with programming, he was well placed to do well in the fast-moving world of the internet. In his youth, his views on technology had been very different. While he was certain that the housing market was not going to recover, he believed with equal unfounded certainty that there was plenty of scope to make money easily by engaging with technology. Neither belief was based on anything but his own feelings – a belief based on a belief. Which is why he'd put forward his ideas on algorithms for more advanced search engines to groups of venture capital investors, but after being rejected, he turned his back on his own ideas. He formed the view that since he had been rejected, the world of technology was clearly not for him. Instead of following through and going somewhere else with his ideas, he put them behind him and adopted an 'I know better' stance, even when close friends told him that his ideas could be worth a fortune. What makes matters worse is that Alan didn't just go to the developers with ideas, but had burned the midnight oil to work up fully functional projects. He was a gnat's whisker away from becoming a dot-com millionaire, but blew it by lacking the commitment to follow through. To add insult to injury, John, a younger colleague of Alan's, who wasn't nearly as talented, did follow through – and keep going. He now splits his time between his ocean-side house in Maui and his offices in Silicon Valley in California. His children surf after school and benefit from a life of financial well-being. John also accepts unreservedly that Alan was a talent to be reckoned with, and can't understand why such a bright bloke is still teaching the same curriculum year after year to adolescents who are more intent on using the products Alan should have had a hand in creating than listening to his classes. Yet again, the success formula would have pushed him over the 'win' line, but poor old Alan didn't have the formula.

If you want to avoid being like 'poor old Alan', then take note of the formula. Everyone can – to a greater or lesser extent – change their future by applying the formula. It doesn't guarantee success, but it does suggest one of two outcomes: either you will achieve your goal, or you will die trying – either way, you will always be heading in the direction *you* want to go. You don't need to be a 'poor old Alan'; all you need is a clear destination and an understanding of how to remain committed to getting there. Without clear direction and at least a destination in mind you won't have the strength of character to take on the challenges that will get in your way, but with clarity and determination the journey itself can be an extraordinary adventure.

> Everyone can ~ to a greater or lesser extent ~ change their future by applying the formula.

When Christopher Columbus set out on his epic journey, he got to the Canary Islands and thought he was somewhere else entirely, then he ended up in America, thinking it was Japan, but who cares? At least he got there, at least he has left a legacy, and at least he did something worthwhile with his life. At least he had the commitment to see something through. The formula isn't new. It wasn't even new when Columbus used it. The formula works, so make it work for you.

Psychological research points strongly to the idea that 'emotional desire' is linked to commitment because to achieve something new always requires a person to do something new – and no one does anything new without wanting to do it. However, there is more to successfully achieving goals than simply deciding to have them.

Five of the most common reasons why goal setting fails are:

1. The goal is set too low. There's not enough challenge required, it doesn't matter very much or it supports the notion of low self-esteem and so is best ignored.

2. The goal is set too high. Unachievable goals either cause a person to lose sight of reality and begin believing their own rhetoric, until finally it becomes clear that the goal will never be reached, or the goal is so out of touch with reality that it's not even worth trying for.

(Psychologists often refer to the standard of 'perfection' as being the least likely to be attained because instinctively the person concerned knows that perfection is unattainable.) The goal that's set too high can cause a person to reflect on their own esteem and find themselves lacking, and therefore feel ill-inclined to attempt to reach it, or they may simply fear the blame associated with failure if they set out to try.

3. The goal becomes part of a bigger issue that isn't always relevant to the person concerned. In other words, they may set out to achieve something big: within that big thing are goals that need to be achieved, but failing to separate them out and see them clearly means they don't get addressed. So the person fails, not just at the little goals but also the big one too.

4. Goal success relies on something other than you. When people hold themselves accountable for things they can't control they will almost always be disappointed. They become frustrated and can easily reach the erroneous conclusion that they are failing. They are not failing; they simply failed to set an achievable and controllable goal.

5. Goals are not about an end result but are about a means of getting there. A goal to 'do better' isn't a useful goal because it's an end result. A person may end up doing a little better but still not being happy with the result. The 'what for' behind the goal needs to be determined before you can consider the 'hows' necessary to get there.

Here's how to avoid letting go of your goals:

1   If you ever forget that your whole world is some aspect of 'memory', then you won't remember what to do to be successful. I have a particular way of thinking about memory that people have found useful. It suggests that all the unconscious can be thought of as being 'memory' — not my idea by the way but supported by renowned psychiatric expert Giulio Tononi.* By thinking of our unconscious as memory, it's possible to use it to help make better decisions. My approach is to think about this memory in three ways: the obvious one, memories of the past; less obvious is memory that allows us to understand the present; counter-intuitively the third is the memory of what the future could be like — you may call it a vision, or imagination, but I prefer to call it 'future memory'! Therefore, past memory consists of experiences you should learn from, current memory is what you're experiencing now (and it will be coloured by your past experiences), and your decisions will be heavily influenced by the third aspect of memory — your future memory. This is your imagination, your creativity, your means of pulling together your past experiences, the experience of others and your current situation, and your way of making decisions that will take you in the direction you want to go. Without future memory, you are on a journey: you may have a satnav, but you're not giving it a destination to head for. That destination and imagined future will never be certain; it's just your best guess at this time, and it's OK to change it, if you have to, as you go along. Without a future memory that serves you well, you may end up with an unintended one that doesn't. By relying so much on your response to the past and the present it will make you certain about a future that doesn't serve you and isn't what you want. It will be a future that does not utilise your strengths and does not give you your best opportunities. Be certain about your future memory, no matter how many times you may have

---

*   A neuroscientist and psychiatrist at the University of Wisconsin, speaking at the World Science Festival. For more, see: Giulio Tononi and Gerald M. Edelman, 'Consciousness and Complexity', *Science*, (1998) 2820(5395): 1846–1851.

to change it, because the one thing you *can* be certain about is that you are trying to do the best you can and make the most of whatever's available.

2   Situations happen, and some of them can be crappy; that's just the way life is. You, however, do not need to respond to life's challenges as if some unseen entity has it in for you personally. As far as I know, there is no entity and nothing 'has it in for you', except you yourself. You will become your biggest enemy if you allow circumstances to dictate the way you feel. You need to be careful what you allow yourself to accept as true. If you believe the government is out to get you, other road users want to kill you, or your boss wants to use and abuse you, then you will give off so many negative vibes whenever an official is near that they'll assume you have something to hide and you'll end up being questioned; you will drive so defensively that you'll cause an accident; and you will annoy your boss so much that any chance you might have had at promotion will be gone – and it will all be your own fault, so be careful what you allow yourself to think.

3   Reflect on your decisions every day. The most successful people in the world either get up earlier or stay up later than most other people. They still get a proper night's sleep, but they make time to reflect: they go for a run, meditate, or simply take the time to think about the decisions they've made and what they now want to do about them. Some they will ignore and let ride; others they will adjust and guide in the direction they want them to go; and some they will change completely. They stay on top by being ruthless, not necessarily with other people, but with themselves. They are their own coach, their own counsellor, and their own guru, and they can be those things because they give themselves time to reflect on the daily decisions they make. You may not want to be the next Richard Branson, but I bet you don't want to be a failed wannabe either. It's in your own hands: take the time to reflect and you'll make better decisions and be constantly rewriting your own story, but if you pretend you don't have the time to reflect, you'll also start pretending that your knee-jerk reaction to events is the 'right' one, and you'll start believing your own story. Trust me, that would be a mistake.

And finally ...

... how to avoid being a loser

WTF just happened to my life?

After each story I've added a short list of actions that you can take to avoid being a loser and to learn from other people's mistakes. What follows now are these ninety actions stripped from the stories and listed here (in no particular order). I'd like you to scroll through them and ask yourself the most important question that comes with all this:

Am I doing anything that might cause me to be a loser?

Ask yourself that question as you read through the list, and you'll know what you have to do. I hope you have fun doing it!

1   Accept that mistakes are going to happen, and man up when they do. The real regret is not over the initial mistake, but your response when it happens. If you get stuck on the idea that it shouldn't have happened, and pretend that embarrassing stuff never happens to anyone, then you will end up regretting the way you behave. A child may stamp their feet and scream the house down because something happens that they can't deal with, but you are not a toddler any more. Behave in that way and you'll look like a child.

2   Ask better questions of, and about, each other. Some people take years to properly get to know each other, and by the time they do, they realise they don't like what they know. All you need to do is ask smarter questions: what do you want out of life? What would your perfect week/home/family/future/retirement etc. look, sound or feel like? What do you really want to avoid happening to you? What irritates you most in another person? What sexual fantasies do you have that you are scared to share? (OK, maybe not that last one, but you get the idea.) The more you know about another person and the more they really know about you, the more able you are to clear your mind and make a better judgement about your compatibility.

3   Ask yourself, am I using my strengths to make myself happy and raise my standards beyond being merely good? If I choose to believe that I can be great at certain aspects of my life, what can I do to start on that path? And if 'great' were to become my personal standard for everything in life, how different would my life be?

4   Be at your best by recognising your strengths and working on them. We all have strengths, but often take them for granted. People can get so caught up in worrying about what they *haven't* got that they forget all the good things that are already theirs. Strengths often go underutilised or unnoticed for years, which is a waste, so identify your strengths, figure out if there's any way you can utilise them even more, then start using them. It doesn't matter if you're not sure how to use them more: just start trying anyway, and you'll learn as you go along.

5   Be clear about the difference between renting and buying assets and liabilities. Years ago my dad earned a bit of extra cash by working as a catalogue agent. That meant taking a printed catalogue of goods around his friends and family, from which they could buy goods and pay for them weekly, rather than all at once. They would buy cheap shoes that — with luck — would last six months, and pay for them over that same period. They paid the basic price, plus interest, and so were actually borrowing the money to buy the goods. Rarely were the goods reclaimed if the money wasn't paid, because the agent made sure the money came in, but technically they could have been. Today people rarely 'buy' their new (or even second-hand) car. They do a lease deal. They pay some money as a deposit and then pay an amount each month over a given period before having to hand the car back. They rent the car. The trouble is, most people don't sit in their new car and acknowledge they're in a rental; they talk about their new car as if it really is. It's not; it's rented. Buying a new house isn't acquiring an asset until you've paid for it. The bank owns it until your final payment; until then, those payments are a liability. Get real about what's yours and what's on the never-never.

6   Be clear about the identity you hold for yourself and whether your behaviours are consistent with it. If you see yourself as being a caring friend, is that what you do? If you call yourself a terrific boss, are you acting like one? If you believe you want to get the most out of life, is that the way you are living?

7   Be clear about where you are right now. Having some debt is necessary — after all, very few people get to own their own home without having a mortgage. Clarity regarding your financial situation is essential if you want to stay in control. Most people fear their finances, and often for good reason. What they then tend to do is either see things as much worse than they really are, or much better than they really are. The answer is not to see things as better or worse than they are, but simply as they are. Embrace the truth. By doing this, you will ask better questions and will live with the reality of your finances. That will feel much better than the alternative.

8   Be clear about your intention each time you use a credit card. You will notice a huge difference in your buying habits if your intention is to pay off your credit card in full

each month, as opposed to building up a debt. No one can make this choice about intent except you. Even if your credit cards are maxed out right now, it doesn't prevent you from intending to pay off what you spend. If you pay off more than the minimum each month, then at some point the debt will be no more. If your intent is to clear your credit cards, then every time you get a bonus or a little extra money you'll feel good about using it to pay off a bit more and eat into your debt. Hold the intention to get yourself sorted, and you will.

9 Be on message all the time; to be 'on message' you need to know what the message should be. You need to know what you are trying to say and what you want other people to see and hear. Once you have clarified what that message is, it's up to you to look at all the material you put out, all the conversations you have, and all the promises you make. You decide what needs to happen to be 'on message', so it's up to you to keep your communication in alignment with your message.

10 Be on the top of your game: you owe it to yourself to be the best you can be. The first person you let down won't be your client; it will be you, if you allow yourself to lag behind your own potential. Everyone has different potential so don't go assuming that anything is possible, but you can assume that you are unlikely to have reached your full potential just yet. Think about your own potential and ask yourself just how good could you be if nothing was preventing you from being at your best? Once you've figured that out you should recognise that whatever you are achieving right now is probably falling short of what you could be. If so, there must be something getting in the way of you reaching that potential. You can't reach your potential if you don't look for those barriers, but you also can't be on the top of your game if you pretend someone else's game is linked to achieving your potential. It's not. You are in control of being at your best, no matter what mistakes you've made or what crazy investments you might have made. You own your potential.

11 Be prepared to change your mind. If you were driving somewhere and realised you were heading the wrong way, not only would you be prepared to change direction, but you'd also be ready to retrace your steps until you found the point at which you went wrong.

Driving your life is no different; you can either pretend that the road you are on will be OK as long as you look at it through a different window, or you can see it for what it is, and change.

12 Be prepared to take action yourself as well as demand action from others. Being misunderstood is as much about energy and enthusiasm as it is about what you are asking to be done. It's common knowledge that 'it ain't what you say it's the way you say it' that matters — and nothing speaks louder or with more resonance than actually taking action yourself. You can tell your children to keep the house tidy, but notice how much faster they take notice if you are seen tidying wherever you go. Leading by example isn't a pithy phrase; it's a means of getting your instructions carried out without misunderstanding.

13 Be realistic: you're going to die one day, that much you can be sure of, but does that day need to be sooner rather than later? You have the power to identify and change any behaviours that put you into a higher risk category. It is valuable to recognise that by doing nothing about them, you are doing something; you are actively saying 'it's OK for me to die sooner than I have to.' If that is true, then knock yourself out and get on with it because ultimately it is your choice, but if it is not true then, for your own sake, act now.

14 Be the friend you want to have. Instead of looking for people to be your friend, seek instead to behave in a way that demonstrates you are already a friend to them. Friendship does not happen because a person presses a button on a mobile device to 'accept' you; it happens because a person feels drawn to you for good reasons. You may share values, you may share some interests, you stimulate each other, and, most of all, you trust each other.

15 Be true to yourself and address any critical weaknesses. We all have weaknesses, and it's a mistake to focus on them at the expense of your strengths. However, if any of those weaknesses are going to stop you from being successful, then you had better recognise them, and quickly. Not only must you know what they are, but you must then do something about them. Make a plan and get on with it. If you are not sure what the plan should be,

then just pick an approach and go with it. If it's not the right one, you'll find out soon enough, and then you can switch to the correct one.

16 Be your own spin doctor. Even if your product isn't the best in the world, it doesn't stop you from being the best *you* you can be. A private contractor, advisor or consultant is successful because he or she meets, and continues to meet, the expectations of the people doing the hiring. They care more about you meeting ~ or exceeding ~ their expectations than they do about anything else, which means establishing (conscious and unconscious) expectations must be your first priority. If you are not a world-famous guru on your subject, make sure your web page doesn't make you out to be. If you are an expert in just one aspect of business, don't claim via your literature and online presence that you are an expert on all aspects of business, because if you do, you'll be caught out, even if your clients aren't trying to catch you out.

17 Become conscious of what you do, and how you do it. The end result comes about because of a combination of behaviours that you must do. You don't own the result; you own the ingredients that make up the result, but it's always up to you to put them together.

18 Believe in yourself enough to make your plans real. You get one shot at this life, to do with it what you please, and if you don't take that opportunity then shame on you. If you want something, then find a way to start making it happen, because if you don't make a start then you have zero chance of ever finishing.

19 Confidence is a feeling. Imagine there's a party going on. In one room people are politely talking about world events (boring); in another there are people dancing (fun); in another there are dark corners with sexy goings-on (great fun). Imagine you couldn't get to the party, but set up a video camera there instead. If it had been fixed in the first room you might not have been that bothered about missing it; if it was in the second room, it would stimulate a different feeling, and the third ~ well, different again. But here's the thing ~ it was all the same party. It's not what's happening that frames our confidence, but what we imagine is happening by how we frame it. Confidence is 'knowing that you know' no matter what the context or situation. Imagine that you are asked to talk to a

stranger about something you are very familiar with. For example, perhaps you are good at making apple pies and are asked to explain how you make one. That shouldn't be a problem, should it? However, imagine that the person asking you is a top-class baker, a Mary Berry or a Paul Hollywood, and not only that but you are being filmed at the same time and broadcast to millions. Are you confident now? Maybe. If you are imagining yourself talking through your memory of making a great apple pie and are focused on the facts that you are confident you know, then it isn't likely to be a problem, but if you start to imagine something different then there will be. If you imagine that the expert is already criticising you in their head, or that some of the millions watching are doubting your methods for apple pie making then might you start to doubt what you know? It is this doubt that causes a lack of confidence because your imagination is stronger and more powerful in controlling your thoughts than you might think.

20 Create your own alter ego. Superman needed Clark Kent and Batman, Bruce Wayne, but Superman was always Superman beneath those horn-rimmed glasses, and Bruce Wayne was still himself behind the black mask. In real life as well as in comic fantasies, people may find it helpful to create an alternative version of themselves that they know will perform better in certain situations.

21 Deal with tough stuff before it gets that way. It's no secret that life throws rocks in the road of blissful happiness, so why make talking about them taboo? You don't make bad stuff happen by talking about how you intend to deal with it; you make it happen by worrying about it and saying nothing until it's too late. Talk about it up-front and agree how you want to deal with it before it happens — not when it's already a problem.

22 Does your plan mean you're doing something that you like and that does you good? Does it lead to producing something that others will like and that will do them good too? Stamping your foot and demanding that the world treats you better is not going to work. Having a flexible plan means not just having enthusiasm, but enthusing other people too. You have to light their fire by engaging them in something they like.

23 Does your plan have wider implications that serve the greater good? Staying on course with your flexi-plan means that it has to be sustainable, and that means it has to do

more than feed you and make a profit. That'll work for a while, but if what you produce doesn't have a lasting value, then you won't last either. Solar lights in a rainforest may sound like a great idea — unless you've actually been to a rainforest, that is. It rains. It has tree canopies that are higher than a block of flats, and it is dark most of the time, where you'd like it to be light. Whatever you do has to have a sustainable value for you to have a sustainable value too.

24 Don't be a pain in the arse when you don't get your own way, even if you truly believe you have been wronged. Instead, get over it, and get over it quickly. If someone has wronged you, then trying to wrong them in return won't help. Not only do two wrongs not make a right; they cause people to get fired, and can really mess up their careers. Remember, you're never going to be at your best when you are disappointed and frustrated, so give yourself space, and take some time to reflect on how to make the most of your situation. If you do go into battle you're not going to win, and when the dust settles the biggest loser will be you, so don't do it.

25 Don't mistake fear for friendship. It can happen anywhere, not just at work: when people appear to become your friends because they fear that if they are not, they will be in danger; in danger of being left out of a group, in danger of being singled out and picked on, in danger of being left out of gossip, or the unspecified danger of a feeling that just seems to push a person into 'sucking up' to someone who, in other circumstances, they might despise.

26 Don't be thrown by changes in circumstances. It's funny when you hear a child say, 'Don't watch me, I can't do it when you watch,' but it's not at all amusing for an adult to act the same way. Do what you need to do, wherever you need to do it.

27 Embrace the concept of JFDI — just flipping do it (or words to that effect). JFDI is meant to suggest diving in without a thought for the consequences: to stop procrastinating and simply get on with it. If you want something, then it's up to you to make it happen. Often that means taking lots of small steps rather than one giant leap, so even if you can't yet see how to make your dreams come true, that's no reason to stop you taking a step towards them. Even a tiny step is better than no step at all.

28 Everyone needs friends. We don't need many, but we do all need some. Friends are people you can trust, which means they have to be consistent and reliable in their connection with you. They must therefore share some aspects of your life that go beyond work, or when the day comes that you go your way and they go theirs and the work goes, they will be gone forever. You need to respect them, and they you, because you share important values and beliefs, or the moment something comes along to challenge your friendship it will be gone. They need to feel close to you, which means they share things with you in the belief that what they tell you stays with you, but if that level of intimacy isn't achieved or is faked, as soon as they realise it the friendship is gone. Finally, they need to know that you are in the friendship as much for what you can give as for what you can gain, and you need to feel that too. If you don't, that friendship will be gone.

29 Find someone who is an example of how you would like to be, and then ask yourself if it's possible for you to do whatever it is they do. Of course, this means you have to have a way of knowing what they do, so choosing somebody you see on the way to work, or who you've admired from afar in Starbucks, is going to be a challenge. 'Excuse me, I read this great book that had me ask myself way better questions, and one of them means I've got to know how you manage to stay in such good shape' is probably one of the worst chat-up lines in history and may get you arrested, so be smart about who you choose as your 'exemplar'.

30 Get over the fact that you are being judged every moment of every day. Your partner will judge you, your kids will judge you, your co-workers will judge you, and as sure as eggs are eggs your boss will judge you too. So no matter how good you were yesterday, no matter how great your CV looks, you had better perform today, right here, right now.

31 Good ideas are ten a penny, but great ideas are rare. Good ideas often don't stand up to closer scrutiny and the harsh spotlight of objective feedback, whereas great ideas stand up to the closest investigation and the most determined criticism. Therefore, invite criticism and encourage research and investigation, because it is better to know in advance that something may not work as well as you hope it will than find out after you have invested your time — and cash — into the idea.

And finally ...
how to avoid
being a loser

32 Hang on to your friends even when they don't agree with you. Friendship and support will matter most to you when things go wrong. It's not difficult to find people to celebrate with you when you are successful, but it's tough to find real friends when your world falls apart. Good friends are a way of protecting yourself from yourself, so that if things get really bad and go terribly wrong you have people who care enough about you to stick with you, even when you're at your worst.

33 Have you got your own flexible plan? Having a fixed plan is like trying to drive from London to Leith using only one route. When a road is blocked, you're in trouble. If this happens more than once, you may start wondering why you wanted to go to Leith in the first place. You may get so frustrated with such a rubbish plan that getting as far as Luton starts to look like a win, and you give up on the rest of the journey. If you set out with a goal and give up on the way, you have to ask yourself what you're missing.

34 At work, how might you add even more value, and add to your own value simultaneously? This does mean eventually asking for more money, more responsibility, more *something*. However, you should only do this at the appropriate time and in the appropriate place. If you don't have performance appraisals with your boss, then arrange one. If your performance reviews are appraisals, then get that bit over with before talking about the future and all the value you want to add. If you don't have a plan for yourself, then you can be pretty sure that someone else will. I don't know about you, but I'd rather be monitoring how I'm doing on my own plan than trying to figure out how I'm fitting into someone else's plan.

35 How much value are you really adding to your company? You may not be married to the firm, but you do have a symbiotic relationship with it. Your company can't function without you — at least, until they replace you or get another employee to cover your work. You can't function without them, unless someone else is paying you and giving you opportunities to advance your career. That means you must ensure they want you, and the best way to do that is to give them what they are paying you for ... and just a little bit more. The chances are that simply being more aware of what you are doing to add value will help you add even more.

36 How special do you feel? Be careful how you think about this: feeling special for a crappy reason isn't really feeling special at all. 'I'm special because no one could be as stupid as I am' is, first, probably not true (you've no idea how many really stupid people there are out there). Second, that's not what I mean by special. I mean special in the 'Wow, I'm actually amazing and wonderful in my own quirky way' sort of special, not any other kind. So be careful.

37 If you are honest, there's only one person you can't lie to – yourself. Even if it takes a while to recognise it, we all know that feeling we get when something just doesn't feel right. That's the feeling you should be looking for when it comes to raising offspring. It's not a problem if you feel it and then do something to (a) recognise what's causing it, and then (b) fix it. It is a problem if you ignore it.

38 If you are true to yourself, then you are likely to be true to your children. Have you asked yourself the tough questions about what you want for yourself out of life, and what you want for them? If not, what's stopping you? The clearer you are about what you want, the more likely it is that you can figure out what to do about it.

39 If you blame something – or someone – else for your own lack of achievement, you are fooling no one but yourself. Taking responsibility for what you do and the results you get is the key to changing those things that are not working for you. Start with the reality of your results and analyse them; take on board those things you like about the results you have achieved and notice what you did to secure them, then identify all those things you do not like and identify what you have done to secure those too. If you allow yourself to slip into 'blaming', the exercise will fail, and it will not help you, so man up and focus.

40 If you ever forget that your whole world is some aspect of 'memory', then you won't remember what to do to be successful. I have a particular way of thinking about memory that people have found useful. It suggests that all the unconscious can be thought of as being 'memory' – not my idea by the way but supported by renowned psychiatric expert Giulio Tononi. By thinking of our unconscious as memory, it's possible to use it to help make better decisions. My approach is to think about this memory in three ways: the obvious one, memories of the past; less obvious is memory that allows us to understand

And finally ...
how to avoid
being a loser

the present; counter-intuitively the third is the memory of what the future could be like — you may call it a vision, or imagination, but I prefer to call it 'future memory'! Therefore, past memory consists of experiences you should learn from, current memory is what you're experiencing now (and it will be coloured by your past experiences), and your decisions will be heavily influenced by the third aspect of memory — your future memory. This is your imagination, your creativity, your means of pulling together your past experiences, the experience of others and your current situation, and your way of making decisions that will take you in the direction you want to go. Without future memory, you are on a journey: you may have a satnav, but you're not giving it a destination to head for. That destination and imagined future will never be certain; it's just your best guess at this time, and it's OK to change it, if you have to, as you go along. Without a future memory that serves you well, you may end up with an unintended one that doesn't. By relying so much on your response to the past and the present it will make you certain about a future that doesn't serve you and isn't what you want. It will be a future that does not utilise your strengths and does not give you your best opportunities. Be certain about your future memory, no matter how many times you may have to change it, because the one thing you can be certain about is that you are trying to do the best you can and make the most of whatever's available.

41 If you had a crystal ball that showed you you'd be successful, then you would be much more likely to step up. A little like if you knew in advance what the lottery numbers were going to be, then you might just buy a ticket. Billions of people all over the world play anyway, even though they don't know what the numbers are, in the hope that they might be lucky. Often the cost of a lottery ticket is worth the weekly hope that comes with it: maybe this week it'll be my numbers? Maybe it's my time? Some people argue that playing the lottery is a waste of money; they argue that each time they *don't* buy a ticket, the money they would have spent goes to buying something they know they want and know they will be able to afford one day. Their certainty about their future is a bigger emotional attraction than the lottery player's eternal hope. What they have in common is a dream for the future: they aren't caught up in today's problems, but are dreaming about the benefits a new tomorrow could bring.

42 If you make a mistake and behave in a way that doesn't meet your own standards, admit it. Acknowledge it and change your behaviour to meet the standards you want for yourself. Don't lower your standards to match your own poor behaviour, because if you do you will live to regret it.

43 If you make a mistake and don't know what to do, do *something* and you will be fine – as long as what you do is positive and takes you closer to fixing things. Trust your instincts: if you feel the need to apologise, then say sorry. If you sense that you've hurt someone's feelings, then ask them if you have. If you need help, then ask for it before it's too late. It doesn't matter how self-reliant or macho you think you are; if you made a mistake then it's your mess to clean up, and if that means seeking support then just do it. People will respect you all the more for keeping your eye on the end goal and not getting caught up with your ego.

44 If you treat children like a borrowed item that has to be tended to and one day given back, then you might avoid making parenting all about you. It's all about focus. If a person is focused on outcome, then it's less likely they'll get caught up with irrelevant issues. Boasting about a kid's brilliance is an 'issue'. Helping a kid become brilliant is an 'outcome'.

45 It may be hackneyed, but I'm saying it anyway: start with your own end in mind. Set your own standards, not by the minimum you can get away with, but by what you'd like to have happen to you. Life will put all manner of barriers in the way of personal happiness, but it's madness to put barriers of your own making in your way by setting personal standards that do not serve you well. If you want a future aimlessly pushing a shopping trolley around and collecting empty tin cans, then set unattainable standards, knowing that you will fail, but if that's not what you want then start getting realistic now; don't wait.

46 Know what you want and why you want it. The more clearly you articulate what you want and the outcome it needs to produce, the better; but that's still not enough. To check meanings, you have to ask what the other person thinks you mean, what they think you are asking for, and what they think the outcome you want looks, sounds and feels like.

And finally ...
how to avoid
being a loser

If you don't ask the right questions, then you should expect to get something different, something you weren't hoping for.

47 Let go of perfection, because all it will do is hold you back. Nothing a human being does in life is perfect, so it follows that your plans won't be perfect either. Flaws are a necessary part of your journey: you don't just plan to go through the motions; you plan to achieve things along the way, such as good feelings, kindness, love, helping your children be the best they can be, actually getting round to having children at all, and all those other things you want to be able to look back on when the time comes and say 'At least I did that.' So give yourself a kick in the pants if necessary, and start turning your plans into something real. No one cares if they're not perfect, and no one but you really cares if you do them at all, so you have to make them happen for *you*, not for anyone else.

48 Listen to the people you care about, respect or love; they are most likely to actually care about you and have your best interests at heart. So, if they say 'you're going to kill yourself doing that', don't ignore them. At the very least, ask what it is about your behaviour that's causing them to be concerned about you. The ultimate arrogance is to ignore everyone else's opinion and think that you know best; the ultimate irony is when you drop dead before your time.

49 Listen to your inner voice. We all have one, but it will be drowned out by life if you never give it a chance to be heard. Anyone who tells you there's no such thing as an inner voice is probably the kind of person who lives amid constant noise: they move from real conversations to being distracted by the radio; put the TV on as soon as they get home, without even really listening to it; and don't give themselves even a moment of quiet contemplation. Your inner voice could be screaming at you to see things in a different way, but if you don't give yourself the opportunity to hear it then you are likely to remain in ignorance, and may fail to live the life you really want.

50 Listen to how you talk to other people. Are you respectful, are you patient, are you at pains to understand what they mean, what their intention is, and if you are achieving your outcome? If you hear yourself being less than respectful, then you have a problem.

You have a problem, not anyone else. It's not someone else's job to put up with your lack of communication skills, make allowances for you, or agree with you when they don't. If you force people to agree with you, then you can be sure that they're only paying lip service and at the first opportunity they will find a way around it.

51 Look around you and see how the people closest to you react to you. Are they at ease and relaxed, do they meet your eye, and do they carry on with whatever they were doing when you walk into the room? If you sense any tension, a lack of eye contact or any indication that people are avoiding you, then you need to pay attention. You need to start asking what you are doing to cause this. Notice that I said what *you* are doing, and not what *their* problem is: this is your problem, your behaviour and your state of mind that's causing other people to respond negatively to you. It's therefore up to you to figure out what you are doing and change it.

52 Be flexible when things aren't working out. If you hear yourself saying: 'I've told him/her already, and it still isn't done', then stop doing what you're doing, because it isn't working. Instead of getting uptight ~ or, worse, giving the same instruction again but this time louder ~ start being flexible. Do something different. If this approach doesn't work, try something different again, over and over again until it does. Of course, that doesn't necessarily mean persevering with the same person. One of your flexible approaches may be to fire somebody. The point is that the only way your instructions can be misunderstood is if you let them be. So don't.

53 Make sure you know that something about you is special. Now you know, ask yourself, what am I doing that helps other people feel special too? What's the best way to feel good about doing the right thing and remaining special? How do I incorporate helping others to feel special, doing the right thing, and making sure I stay special too, into my everyday activities?

54 Nothing is ever over, even when the fat lady appears to have sung her last note. You may have been told you are wonderful, you may have done a good job, you may look the part and say all the right things ~ but if you don't demonstrate the quality and performance that someone is expecting, then you will pay the price. There is no reason for you to

forget who you are and what you know, except if you lose concentration because you lack preparation and practice. No performer is 'brilliant' the first time out; practice isn't just about memory, it's about expectation and the uncovering of tiny distinctions that other people don't see. The more familiar you become with whatever you need to demonstrate, the more comfortable and confident you will become, and the more you will recognise the appropriateness of whatever support material you use. You will get it right first time, every time, because it won't really be your first time; professionals make sure of that.

55 People lie. People who want something from you lie even more. So when they tell you you're the best thing since sliced bread, you had better take it with a pinch of salt or you are setting yourself up to be sucker-punched. As soon as you don't give them what they want, they will find your weak spot and they will use it. If they don't, then consider it a bonus. It is not an excuse for you to be unprepared.

56 Potential isn't the same as success. To make your potential materialise, you have to recognise what's getting in the way of you achieving it, even if the biggest barrier is you. You must keep your ego in check, because if it isn't it will stop you dead in your tracks. Instead, you must imagine what your realised potential will look like, sound like and feel like. Then, and only then, can you ask the toughest question of all: 'Is what I'm doing now taking me closer to, or further away from, where I really want to go?'

57 Pretending that you have goals and objectives but not really meaning them is a meaningless activity; it affects only you, the people you care about and your future. Be clear about what you really want, and not what you think you *ought* to want. There is a huge difference between your own authentic aspirations and those you feel you must achieve to prove to other people that you are OK. Be OK with your own goals and your own ambitions.

58 Recognise that if one person like you can do something amazing, then so can you. Not everyone is lucky enough to be born into a society where everyone goes to school, and where having your own mobile phone is considered a necessity by the time you're ten. The problems with reaching your full potential are going to be different in the Borneo rainforest than they are in a Birmingham suburb. So comparing the two is irrelevant. Comparing the lives of people from similar backgrounds and similar circumstances can't tell you everything you need to know about your potential, but can offer up useful clues. Luck is simply the meeting of opportunity with preparation. So be prepared.

59 Recognise that liking is as important as loving. Love is a wonderful thing. I think most people agree with that, but ask them to define what love is, and you'll get a different answer from just about everyone you ask. Love is hard to pin down. Are there different types of love? Is loving someone and being 'in love' different? Does love blossom or is it just there? However, we all have a reasonably common reference when it comes to liking someone. We either do or we don't. They are either our friend or they are not. Things like trust, honesty, friendliness, compassion, reliability, intimacy — not in the sexual sense, but meaning the sharing of secrets, and just being able to 'rub along' together in companionable silence — are the building blocks of friendship, and long-term successful relationships need them.

60 Recognise that possibility exists everywhere, and that success is not a linear path. It is not possible to pick a future, and draw a line between where you are now and where you would like to be, hoping that you can follow the line like some kind of pathway to success. Everyone travels on a winding road; it may sometimes loop back on itself and appear to be taking you further away from where you need to be, but knowing that you are doing what's necessary to move you eventually towards your goal will be enough to keep you on the right path.

61 Recognise that what you do is actively shaping the person you are. Human beings develop patterns of behaviour that they can't help repeating. Honestly, we can't help it: if you've ever been to a free seating conference and then left the auditorium for a break, which chair do you go back to? If the conference is for more than one day, which chair do you head for the next day? The same one, right? We are all creatures of habit, and we like patterns, so think about whether your patterns and habits are helping or hindering you. Is what you are doing right now taking you closer to, or further away from, what you really want?

62 Recognise that yesterday can't be changed – but today can. Why do so many people become fixated on what's happened rather than using their time to figure out what they want to happen next? Guilt about mistakes, shame about bad decisions, and the fear of being found out are just some of the reasons why people spend more time looking back than forward.

63 Recognise that you are not the only person in the world with emotions. Everybody has emotions, everyone has needs and desires, and everyone wants to satisfy them. However, if you put your emotional needs before other people's, then you will pay the price. If you are so out of touch with other people's emotions that you don't realise you are subjugating their needs in order to fulfil your own, then you will hurt them. If you hurt them badly enough, they will find a way to hurt you too.

64 Recognise the things that are happening to you as opposed to the things you are making happen. Ignorance is not bliss, because at some point you will become aware of what you have done. The things that happened to you haven't caused you to do whatever you did; they simply provided a background onto which you could act out your own play. The choices you made were yours, and although you may have made them unthinkingly, at some point you must begin to think for yourself.

65 Reflect on your decisions every day. The most successful people in the world either get up earlier or stay up later than most other people. They still get a proper night's sleep, but they make time to reflect: they go for a run, meditate, or simply take the time to think about the decisions they've made and what they now want to do about them. Some they will ignore and let ride; others they will adjust and guide in the direction they want them to go; and some they will change completely. They stay on top by being ruthless, not necessarily with other people, but with themselves. They are their own coach, their own counsellor, and their own guru, and they can be those things because they give themselves time to reflect on the daily decisions they make. You may not want to be the next Richard Branson, but I bet you don't want to be a failed wannabe either. It's in your own hands: take the time to reflect and you'll make better decisions and be constantly rewriting your own story, but if you pretend you don't have the time to reflect, you'll also start pretending that your knee-jerk reaction to events is the 'right' one, and you'll start believing your own story. Trust me, that would be a mistake.

66   Remember that having style is a choice: it's asking yourself 'How do I want to look, and how do I want to behave?' so that you get as close as you can to your ideal. You do style for you, not anyone else, and as long as you know you are doing it for you you'll keep on doing it; do it for someone or something else and why would it last? It's meaningless. Do it for yourself.

67   Remember that time passes even more quickly when we are not paying attention. People let themselves go when they feel comfortable as they are. If you go on holiday for a couple of weeks and stay in one place, time passes quickly as soon as you feel comfortable with where you are, but if you change location two or three times, the holiday will feel like it has lasted way longer — because you were paying attention. Pay attention to the effect that time has on you and your style, and you won't let yourself go.

68   Remember to grow, and change the way you present yourself to the world so that it is consistent with the way you want the world to see you. It's unlikely that you will have the same views, values or priorities, or the same choice of lifestyle at different points in your life. Therefore it is perfectly reasonable for you to reinvent yourself as often as you want to, simply to make the best of who you are at that time. There are people who make their style so consistent that it becomes their identity, and they don't change with fashions or with what's popular at the time. However, those people are rare. For them, they make the best of who they are by being who they are purposefully and with great clarity. As opposed to the person who simply loses an awareness of themselves as they get caught up in life, and who doesn't notice time passing or themselves changing. It's not just about being age-appropriate, or wearing something comfortable. Being the best you can be and presenting yourself to the world in ways that make the most of yourself is an issue for anyone who wants to avoid a 'WTF just happened to my style?' moment.

69   Self-protection is a vital component of survival, whereas approval, on the other hand, is a temporary desire that fulfils a need to connect with other people and feel valued. Everyone needs to feel connected and valued — but not at the risk of self-protection.

And finally ...
how to avoid
being a loser

Therefore, before saying yes to anything, be sure that it is something that you really want to do, not something that you are doing for approval.

70 Situations happen, and some of them can be crappy; that's just the way life is. You, however, do not need to respond to life's challenges as if some unseen entity has it in for you personally. As far as I know, there is no entity and nothing 'has it in for you', except you yourself. You will become your biggest enemy if you allow circumstances to dictate the way you feel. You need to be careful what you allow yourself to accept as true. If you believe the government is out to get you, other road users want to kill you, or your boss wants to use and abuse you, then you will give off so many negative vibes whenever an official is near that they'll assume you have something to hide and you'll end up being questioned; you will drive so defensively that you'll cause an accident; and you will annoy your boss so much that any chance you might have had at promotion will be gone – and it will all be your own fault, so be careful what you allow yourself to think.

71 Start with the premise that you might be wrong rather than the certainty that you are right. Don't lower your levels of confidence or certainty in your own ability, but recognise that you are fallible, you are human, and humans make mistakes.

72 Step back and look at yourself. Reflect on the way you are behaving and the standards you are keeping. Ask yourself if these standards reflect the way you want to live and the life you want to lead. Ask yourself if living to these standards is more or less likely to take you in the direction you want to go.

73 The online world of technology need be no scarier than the real world of loan sharks and huge interest rates. You are not being paranoid if you think that there are people out there who want to get you; there are, and they will if you let them. It's up to you to be aware of what you do and to protect yourself. Don't use passwords that any casual online stalker could figure out easily; don't put financial paperwork into the paper recycling without shredding it if you don't want someone to read it and steal it; and don't allow anyone else to access your mail but you.

74 There's a rule: the more the boss has to prove a case, the less likely it is that the case can be proved. People in positions of power are just people: they are as fallible as anyone else, and sometimes, when you can't believe they've been given their job, they can't believe it either. So there's no need to treat them as if they are the police or that you're in the forces and they can put you on the front line whether you like it or not (unless of course you are in the forces). Their job is to support you to do a better job. Part of that support may be to stop you failing, so you may need them to steer you on occasion, but they are not there for any other reason than to 'be there' for you.

75 Think about what you want your online presence to do. If you want to share what you are up to with the world, then have at it, but please be aware of the potential consequences. If you want to separate your business self from your personal self then you have to do more than just have different accounts, because the bad people are not stupid people, and they will find you.

76 Think of each day with this person you love as being a gift. Imagine what it would be like if they weren't with you, and do everything you can to make sure you play your part in getting on with loving as well as living in the moment. When you treasure every moment, even the ones where you argue or disagree, as something that is meant to be part of your life together, then you will see them for what they really are: a real, genuine gift and something to be treasured. The more love you give, the more you will get, and if for some tragic reason the person you love is taken away from you, then at least when they're gone you will have no regrets.

77 Time doesn't make things better; you do. They say that watching a kettle makes it feel like the water takes ages to boil, but watching that kettle without turning on any heat will have you waiting forever, and it won't even get warm. If you want your mojo back, then you can't wait for life to light a fire under you; you have to light it yourself.

78 Treat your lover as well as you would your best friend, and consider them a partner, not an acquisition. Life partners are not a thing you own; they are their own person. People don't think of their best friends as anything but a person in his or her own right, to be treated with respect. If you want your love to last, then you must treat your lover with at least the same respect you do your best friend. Forget that, and you will suffer the consequences; you will eventually be dumped.

79 Trust your gut — not to tell you what to do, but that it's telling you to investigate further. You can't know what your gut feeling means. It may be that a feeling of dread is trying to tell you not to miss a fabulous opportunity. Equally, a positive gut feeling may be telling you to positively avoid something, and stay in control of your future. The only thing you can be sure of is that you have gut feelings for a reason, and they deserve investigation.

80 What physical shape do you *really* want to be in? Not the shape you would kinda like to have if it wasn't too much trouble, but the shape that you absolutely *have* to have for you to live happily.

81 When in doubt, say what's on your mind. If you ask a question with the express intent of gaining clarity, then you'll unscramble any confusion. It may not be easy or comfortable, but the alternative — bottling it up — can only end badly.

82 When something goes wrong, the first thing to consider is not what you wish had happened instead, but what you want to happen now. You must quickly figure out your best-scenario outcome so that you can start putting out the fires you've started with your mistake. The more fires you kill, the less you'll regret making the mistake, and the less damage will be done.

83 When did you last review the deal you have with your employers? This is not an excuse to demand or beg for a pay rise. That may end up getting you fired anyway, so it's not a great idea. It's a question that makes you re-evaluate whether you are actually doing what you are being paid to do. Not all 'WTF, I just got fired' moments are unfair. There are plenty of employees who get sloppy and take things for granted. They may have appreciated the wonderful benefits and great bonuses when they got the job. They may even work hard and do a great job ... for a while. They may also forget all about that after a few years of being with the company and comparing themselves to people they perceive as being worse than they are. This false sense of security and unappreciative

attitude won't go unnoticed. Then, one day, when it's least expected, the WTF moment will happen — and it'll be no one's fault but their own.

84 When you eat the first thing you see without looking at a menu, then you shouldn't be surprised when it's not to your taste. Like a restaurant is full of different dishes, some of which will be to your taste and some that won't be, so the world is full of potential matches, some of which will be a good fit and some not so much. Imagine how disappointed you'd be if you went to the restaurant convinced that you only have one shot at ordering a meal you'll love, and then when the food came it wasn't all that. How easy would it be to convince yourself to make do, because there might not be another meal choice after this one? I'm not suggesting you need to eat your way through the whole menu, but you do have to open your eyes to the choice. The same is true for finding love. Who knows, you may well be 'fated' to meet the love of your life, but it doesn't hurt to double-check before jumping in with both feet. Be sure to try before you buy, and never be afraid to take a chance, either to wait for the 'right one' or, if it feels like it is right, to take the risk. If you have thought things through then it's probably going to be worth it.

85 When you find a person you truly love, then love them completely. If you can't give your love, it's not because they are doing something wrong, it's because you are either trying to love someone who is not right for you, or you're being controlled by some other unconscious drive that's distracting you. Figure out which it is, and deal with it. If you are not with the right person, then do both of you a big favour and part. However, if you are holding back for any reason then deal with it: get help, talk it through, meditate or do whatever it is you need to do to fix it, because if you don't it will hurt you.

86 When you have a doubt about something, then look for alternatives before accepting anything at face value. Your gut feeling is a part of your brain trying to tell you something; you can't know whether that feeling is telling you that what you are doing is right, or if it's telling you to get the heck out of there because what you are doing is wrong. All you can deduce is that there is 'something' for you to investigate, and it is up to you to figure out what it is and if it is important. Chances are, any worries you have

And finally ...
how to avoid
being a loser

come from the latent suspicion caused by binge-watching crime drama on Netflix, but it's better to probe and be wrong than hear that little voice in your head say 'I told you so.'

87 Who do you know, or know of, who is already the physical shape you want to be, and appears to be able to maintain it without apparent effort? In other words, don't choose somebody who has to have regular coffee enemas or needs to climb mountains to stay fit. Choose somebody relatively 'normal' to aspire to.

88 You don't know everything, so don't pretend that you do. If you don't ask better questions, then you won't get better answers. You only ever get to see your view of everything, so you must step out of your own certainty and step up into accepting someone else's. They may not be any more 'right' than you are, but they have their own point of view and they have as much right to it as you do to yours. It requires some stepping up to be able to let go of your own certainty and accept someone else's, even for a short while, but the benefits of stepping up are that you get to ask much better questions; questions like, 'If I were in their shoes how might I see things differently?' 'When have I been surprised to be wrong in the past?' or even 'How can I use the situation to my advantage even though I wouldn't necessarily choose to be here?' Ask better questions of yourself and you will find that the answers you get are inevitably more helpful.

89 Your future is at risk from disasters of your own making; your current success is no indication of what's to come in your future, nor is your current lack of success. We live in a dynamic world that responds to whatever we do. The more resourceful you allow yourself to be, the more dynamically you'll respond, and the better results you'll end up achieving.

90 It's easy to lose your mojo. For as long as it is less painful to stay as you are, and more painful to look for your mojo, it will stay lost. The trick is to make staying as you are *more* painful than seeking your mojo.

Praise for *WTF Just Happened?*

This is one of those annoying books – annoying in a good way! I found myself relating to so many chapters and my annoyance was that I wished I had read the book before I had experienced many of the WTF moments Martin has highlighted. A thoroughly enjoyable read which I found very relatable – frustratingly relatable at times. Martin offers advice that I could have used during my career as a professional sportsman, in my personal life and also in facing the challenges that life after sport often brings. Although I am not naive enough to think that I won't experience any further WTF moments in my life because I have read this book, I do feel like I am far better placed to face any that may creep up on me in the future, so thank you, Martin.

Leon Lloyd, former Leicester and England rugby international, Director of Switch the Play, Partner at JMAC Capital Partners

As we go through life, ducking and diving the slings and arrows that fire in our direction, we face many WTF moments. Undoubtedly, some of these moments are joyful, ones to cherish and rejoice in. All too often, they are not. These moments, be they of great magnitude or not, can leave us scarred, scared, sad and sceptical. It's how we react to, deal with and move on from these WTF challenges that really counts. Sadly, for some, 'moving on' and learning positively from those experiences, or even avoiding them in the first place, isn't easy. Many will battle on through life (or, tragically, not) lugging all those WTF moments behind them like excess baggage. Enter life coach and psychologist Martin Goodyer.

This is not, he maintains, a self-help book. Heaven knows there are enough of those around. No, writes Goodyer, the self-help bit is up to you. He does, however, draw on a myriad, sometimes complex, range of life stories, with something for everyone to relate to at some point. These stories range from how to avoid putting up with unhappiness, how to avoid saying 'what if' and 'if only', how to avoid missing an open door, how to avoid missing out on life to, finally, the conclusion; how to avoid being a loser.

Take note: the stories, drawn from Goodyer's years of life coaching, are not sugar-coated. The stories, with subsequent suggested actions and strategies, make it possible to alter the course of your own life, move on from the WTF moments and avoid too many WTFs in the future.

This is a practical, common-sense, no-nonsense, easy-to-read work. Goodyer writes with empathy but is plain-speaking, offering strength, encouragement, strategy and reflection in equal measure. It's a sensible toolkit to aid you in altering the course of your life and dealing with those slings and arrows.

Annie Othen, broadcaster and journalist

A very unique perspective on self-development: a fun book to read, littered with pointers and suggestions about 'how not to do it'. Martin's approach is refreshing and the memorable stories he shares empower you to take action to combat common mistakes, unhelpful behaviours and limiting beliefs – hopefully preventing a WTF moment of your own!

Danielle Brown MBE, speaker